CARIBBEAN WRITERS

16

Cricket in the Road

CARIBBEAN WRITERS SERIES

Michael Anthony

CRICKET IN THE ROAD

Introduction by the author

HEINEMANN

IN ASSOCIATION WITH
ANDRE DEUTSCH

Heinemann Educational Books Ltd
22 Bedford Square, London WC1B 3HH
P.O. Box 1028, Kingston, Jamaica
27 Belmont Road, Port of Spain, Trinidad
IBADAN NAIROBI
EDINBURGH MELBOURNE AUCKLAND
HONG KONG SINGAPORE KUALA LUMPUR
NEW DELHI

Heinemann Educational Books Inc.
4 Front Street, Exeter, New Hampshire 03833, USA

ISBN 0 435 98032 7

FOR
SANDRA AND CARLOS

Made and printed in Great Britain by
Richard Clay (The Chaucer Press) Ltd,
Bungay, Suffolk

Contents

✣✣✣

Introduction

I came to writing short stories, in a manner of speaking, by accident. I had always wanted to write, but my first love was poetry. Throughout my childhood years and my early teens I had wanted to become a poet, and by the time I had left school in the 1940s I began to try my hand at verse.

But something happened that diverted my attention towards the short story. Some time in the late 1940s, a Trinidad newspaper started a short story competition and stipulated, among other things, that stories 'must be of a local flavour'. That competition threw up some of the finest pieces of Trinidad writing that I ever saw, and what was new and refreshing to me was the treatment of local themes and the use of the local idiom. It made literature look 'real' to me then.

One of the great incentives of the time was a programme called *Caribbean Voices*, broadcast by the BBC in London. This was a programme of verse and prose to which West Indian writers contributed. A member of the Southern Writers Association had had a short story or two broadcast on the programme, and for this he was revered by us as a being out of this world – so highly did we esteem this sort of success.

Also, at that time, West Indian authors – and they were very few on the ground – were going to England to write, and with the lack of opportunities here in Trinidad I felt like going to try my luck too.

One of the first things I did when I arrived there in December 1954, was to bombard the producer of *Carib-*

bean Voices with a number of poems accompanied by one of my first efforts at writing a short story. Consequently, shortly afterwards, I received a note from the producer of the programme, which said something like this : 'We have given careful consideration to your poems and regret that they are of a light nature and therefore not suitable for this programme. On the other hand, we find your short story promising and intend to use it. We would like to suggest that perhaps you can send us further short stories for consideration.'

I felt crushed by the dismissal of my poems, but elated about what had happened to my story. It was called *The Strange Flower,* and the strangest thing about it is that I neither kept a copy of it, nor said anything about it, until now. But it was the story that really launched me into prose.

The first story I wrote after that was *The Girl and the River*, and this was lucky enough to catch the producer's eye. I wrote *The Girl and the River* with the idea of seeing if I could tell a story I wanted to tell by mixing fact with fiction. I have always been fascinated by this quality of fact in fiction, especially when the base of the story is fact. It seemed to me that a work of fiction based on fact was more meaningful than one that stemmed totally from the imagination. I felt that even if the people directly concerned are dead, the story has some historical significance, especially if it is linked to some recognizable place. Of course this is a matter of opinion.

Anyway, in the case of *The Girl and the River,* I was recollecting the time not many years before when the ferry that plied the Ortoire river was done away with and a brand new steel bridge erected. I used to know the ferryman as he passed to and from my home in Mayaro, and I wondered how he felt to see his job snatched from him. And I knew for a fact that a lot of his partisans in

Ortoire village did not take it too kindly, and were not impressed by new-fangled things such as steel bridges. I felt I would like to say something about his situation, and that story, which appears in this book, was what resulted. After the acceptance of that story I settled down with the main intention of writing for *Caribbean Voices*. At that period I wrote *Cricket in the Road*, *The Village Shop*, and *The Sapodilla Tree*, all based on actual experiences, or at least on situations I knew well. Only very occasionally I spliced in a story that was purely imaginative, like *Peeta of the Deep Sea*, or half-imaginative like *Uncle of the Waterfront*, and *Hibiscus*. At moments I thought I would tap our rich history and write stories like *The Captain of the Fleet*.

But my main desire was always to write about something I actually knew and experienced, and belonging as I do to Mayaro it was only natural that most of my stories should be set there, although all of them have been written in England. There are only two stories set in San Fernando – *Enchanted Alley*, and *The Day of the Fearless* – although I spent a childhood year and many of my adolescent years there. But *Enchanted Alley* was the crystallizing of an idea that led me to write a longer work about the place – *The Year in San Fernando*.

Having described all this, I would like to say that this collection represents my complete work in short stories, because although I have written many others these are the only ones that have 'survived'.

The nine stories in the Heinemann Secondary Readers collection entitled *Sandra Street* are embodied in this work. Most of these short stories have been published in BIM, the Barbados literary magazine, to whom I make grateful acknowledgement.

MICHAEL ANTHONY
Chaguanas, Trinidad

Sandra Street

✣✣✣

Mr Blades, the new teacher, was delighted with the compositions we wrote about Sandra Street. He read some aloud to the class. He seemed particularly pleased when he read what was written by one of the boys from the other side of the town.

'Sandra Street is dull and uninteresting,' the boy wrote. 'For one half of its length there are a few houses and a private school (which we go to) but the other half is nothing but a wilderness of big trees.' Mr Blades smiled from the corners of his mouth and looked at those of us who belonged to Sandra Street. 'In fact,' the boy wrote, '*it* is the only street in our town that has big trees, and I do not think it is a part of our town at all because it is so far and so different from our other streets.'

The boy went on to speak of the gay attractions on the other side of the town, some of which, he said, Sandra Street could never dream to have. In his street, for instance, there was the savannah where they played football and cricket, but the boys of Sandra Street had to play their cricket in the road. And to the amusement of Mr Blades, who also came from the other side of the town, he described Sandra Street as a silly little girl who ran away to the bushes to hide herself.

Everyone laughed except the few of us from Sandra Street, and I knew what was going to happen when school was dismissed, although Mr Blades said it was all a joke

9

and in fact Sandra Street was very fine. I did not know whether he meant this or not, for he seemed very much amused and I felt this was because he came from the other side of the town.

He read out a few more of the compositions. Some of them said very nice things about Sandra Street, but those were the ones written by ourselves. Mr Blades seemed delighted about these, too, and I felt he was trying to appease us when he said that they showed up new aspects of the beauty of Sandra Street. There were only a few of us who were appeased, though, and he noticed this and said all right, next Tuesday we'll write about the other side of the town. This brought fiendish laughter from some of us from Sandra Street, and judging from the looks on the faces of those from the other side of the town, I knew what would happen next Tuesday, too, when school was dismissed. And I felt that whatever happened it wasn't going to make any difference to our side or to the other side of the town.

Yet the boy's composition was very truthful. Sandra Street was so different from the other streets beyond. Indeed, it came from the very quiet fringes and ran straight up to the forests. As it left the town there were a few houses and shops along it, and then the school, and after that there were not many more houses, and the big trees started from there until the road trailed off to the river that bordered the forests. During the day all would be very quiet except perhaps for the voice of one neighbour calling to another, and if some evenings brought excitement to the schoolyard, these did very little to disturb the calmness of Sandra Street.

Nor did the steel band gently humming from the other side of the town. I had to remember the steel band because although I liked to hear it I had to put into my composition that it was very bad. We had no steel bands in Sandra Street, and I thought I could say that this was because we were decent, cultured folk, and did not like the horrible noises of steel bands.

I sat in class recalling the boy's composition again. Outside the window I could see the women coming out of the shops. They hardly passed each other without stopping to talk, and this made me laugh. For that was exactly what the boy had written – that they could not pass without stopping to talk, as if they had something to talk about.

I wondered what they talked about. I did not know. What I did know was that they never seemed to leave Sandra Street to go into the town. Maybe they were independent of the town! I chuckled a triumphant little chuckle because this, too, would be good to put into my composition next Tuesday.

Dreamingly I gazed out of the window. I noticed how Sandra Street stood away from the profusion of houses. Indeed, it did not seem to belong to the town at all. It stood off, not proudly, but sadly, as if it wanted peace and rest. I felt all filled up inside. Not because of the town in the distance but because of this strange little road. It was funny, the things the boy had written; he had written in anger what I thought of now in joy. He had spoken of the pleasures and palaces on the other side of the town. He had said why they were his home sweet home. As I looked at Sandra Street, I, too, knew why it was my home sweet home. It was dull and uninteresting to him but it meant so much to me. It was. . . .

'Oh!' I started, as the hand rested on my shoulder.

'It's recess,' said Mr Blades.

'Oh! . . . yes, sir.' The class was surging out to the playground. I didn't seem to have heard a sound before.

11

Mr Blades looked at me and smiled. 'What are you thinking of?' he said.

He seemed to be looking inside me. Inside my very mind. I stammered out a few words which, even if they were clear, would not have meant anything. I stopped. He was still smiling quietly at me. 'You are the boy from Sandra Street?' he said.

'Yes, sir."

'I thought so,' he said.

What happened on the following Tuesday after school was a lot worse than what had ever happened before, and it was a mystery how the neighbours did not complain or Mr Blades did not get to hear of it. We turned out to school the next morning as if all had been peaceful, and truly, there was no sign of the battle, save the little bruises which were easy to explain away.

We kept getting compositions to write. Mr Blades was always anxious to judge what we wrote but none gave him as much delight as those we had written about Sandra Street. He had said that he knew the other side of the town very well and no one could fool him about that, but if any boy wrote anything about Sandra Street he would have to prove it. And when he had said that, he had looked at me and I was very embarrassed. I had turned my eyes away, and he had said that when the mango season came he would see the boy who didn't speak the truth about Sandra Street.

Since that day I was very shy of Mr Blades, and whenever I saw him walking towards me I turned in another direction. At such times there would always be a faint smile at the corners of his mouth.

I stood looking out of the school window one day thinking about this and about the compositions when again I felt a light touch and jumped.

12

'Looking out?' Mr Blades said.

'Yes, sir.'

He stood there over me and I did not know if he was looking down at me or looking outside, and presently he spoke; 'Hot, eh?'

'Yes,' I said.

He moved in beside me and we both stood there looking out of the window. It was just about noon and the sun was blazing down on Sandra Street. The houses stood there tall and rather sombre-looking, and there seemed to be no movement about save for the fowls lying in the shadows of the houses. As I watched this a certain sadness came over me and I looked over the houses across to the hills. Suddenly my heart leapt and I turned to Mr Blades, but I changed my mind and did not speak. He had hardly noticed that I looked up at him. I saw his face looking sad as his eyes wandered about the houses. I felt self-conscious as he looked at the houses for they no longer were new and the paint had been washed off them by the rains and they had not been repainted. Then, too, there were no gates and no fences around them as there were in the towns, and sometimes, with a great flurry, a hen would scamper from under one house to another leaving dust behind in the hot sun.

I looked at Mr Blades. He was smiling faintly. He saw me looking at him. 'Fowls,' he said.

'There are no gates,' I apologized.

'No, there are no gates.' And he laughed softly to himself.

'Because . . .' I had to stop. I did not know why there were no gates.

'Because you did not notice that before.'

'I noticed that before,' I said.

Looking sharply at me he raised his brows and said slowly: 'You noticed that before. Did you put that in

13

your composition? You are the boy from Sandra Street, are you not?'

'There are more from Sandra Street.'

'Did you notice the cedar grove at the top?' he went on. 'You spoke of the steel band at the other side of the town. Did you speak of the river? Did you notice the hills?'

'Yes.'

'Yes?' His voice was now stern and acid. His eyes seemed to be burning up from within.

'You noticed all this and you wrote about Sandra Street without mentioning it, eh? How many marks did I give you?'

'Forty-five.'

He looked surprised. 'I gave you forty-five for writing about the noises and about the dirty trams of the town? Look!' he pointed, 'Do you see?'

'Mango blossoms,' I said, and I felt like crying out: *'I wanted to show it to you!'*

'Did you write about it?'

'No.' I just wanted to break out and run away from him. He bent down to me. His face looked harder now, though kind, but I could see there was fury inside him.

'There is something like observation, Steve,' he said. *'Observation.* You live in Sandra Street, yet Kenneth writes a composition on your own place better than you.'

'He said Sandra Street was soppy,' I cried.

'Of course he said it was soppy. It was to his purpose. He comes from the other side of the town. What's he got to write on – gaudy houses with gates like prisons around them? High walls cramping the imagination? The milling crowd with faces impersonal as stone, hurrying on buses, hurrying off trams? Could he write about that? He said Sandra Street was soppy. Okay, did you prove it wasn't so? Where is your school and his, for instance?'

14

I was a little alarmed. Funny how I did not think of that point before. 'Here,' I said. 'In Sandra Street.'

'Did you mention that?'

Mercifully, as he was talking, the school bell sounded. The fowls, startled, ran out into the hot sun across the road. The dust rose, and above the dust, above the houses, the yellow of mango blossom caught my eye.

'The bell, sir.'

'Yes, the bell's gone. What's it now – Geography?'

'Yes, sir,' I said. And as I turned away he was still standing there, looking out into the road.

It was long before any such thing happened again. Though often when it was dry and hot I stood at the window looking out. I watched the freedom of the fowls among the tall houses, and sometimes the women talked to each other through the windows and smiled. I noticed, too, the hills, which were now streaked with the blossoms of the poui, and exultantly I wondered how many people observed this and knew it was a sign of the rains. None of the mango blossoms could be seen now, for they had already turned into fruit, and I knew how profuse they were because I had been to the hills.

I chuckled to myself. *There is something like observation, Steve.* And how I wished Mr Blades would come to the window again so I could tell him what lay among the mango trees in the hills.

I knew that he was not angry with me. I realized that he was never angry with any boy because of the parts the boy came from. We grew to like him, for he was very cheerful, though mostly he seemed dreamy and thoughtful. That is, except at composition time.

He really came to life then. His eyes would gleam as he read our compositions and whenever he came to a word he did not like he would frown and say any boy

15

was a sissy to use such a word. And if a composition pleased him he would praise the boy and be especially cheerful with him and the boy would be proud and the rest of us would be jealous and hate him.

I was often jealous. Mr Blades had a passion for compositions, and I was anxious to please him to make up for that day at the window. I was anxious to show him how much I observed and often I noted new things and put them into my compositions. And whenever I said something wonderful I knew it because of the way Mr Blades would look at me, and sometimes he would take me aside and talk to me. But many weeks ran out before we spoke at the window again.

I did not start this time because I had been expecting him. I had been watching him from the corners of my eyes.

'The sun's coming out again,' he said.

'It's cloudy,' I said.

The rains had ceased but there were still great patches of dark cloud in the sky. When the wind blew they moved slowly and cumbersomely, but if the sun was free of one cloud there would soon be another. The sun was shining brightly now, although there was still a slight drizzle of rain, and I could smell the steam rising from the hot pitch and from the galvanized roofs.

'Rain falling sun shining,' Mr Blades said. And I remembered that they said at such times the Devil fought his wife, but when Mr Blades pressed me to tell what I was laughing at I laughed still more and would not say. Then thoughtfully he said, 'You think they're all right?'

'What, sir?'

'In the 'mortelle root.'

I was astonished. I put my hands to my mouth. How did he know?

16

He smiled down at me: 'You won't be able to jump over now.' And the whole thing came back. I could not help laughing. I had put into my composition how I had gone into the hills on a Sunday evening, and how the mango trees were laden with small mangoes, some full, and how there were banana trees among the immortelle and poui. I had written, too, about the bunch of green bananas I had placed to ripen in the immortelle roots and how afterwards I had jumped across the river to the other bank.

'They're all right,' I said, and I pretended to be watching the steam rising from the hot pitch.

'I like bananas,' said Mr Blades. I was sure that he licked his lips as he looked towards the hills.

I was touched. I felt as one with him. I liked bananas, too, and they always made me lick my lips. I thought now of the whole bunch which must be yellow by now inside the immortelle roots.

'Sir . . .' I said to him, hesitating. Then I took the wild chance. And when he answered, a feeling of extreme happiness swept over me.

I remember that evening as turning out bright, almost blinding. The winds had pushed away the heavy clouds, and the only evidence of the rains was the little puddles along Sandra Street. I remember the hills as being strange in an enchanted sort of way, and I felt that part of the enchantment came from Mr Blades being with me. We watched the leaves of the cocoa gleaming with the moisture of the rains, and Mr Blades confessed he never thought there was so much cocoa in the hills. We watched the cyp, too, profuse among the laden mango trees, and the redness of their rain-picked flowers was the redness of blood.

We came to the immortelle tree where I had hidden

the bananas. I watched to see if Mr Blades licked his lips but he did not. He wasn't even watching.

'Sir,' I said in happy surprise, after removing the covering of trash from the bunch. Mr Blades was gazing across the trees. I raised my eyes. Not far below, Sandra Street swept by, bathed in light.

'The bananas, sir,' I said.

'*Bananas!*' he cried, despairingly. 'Bananas are all you see around you, Steve?'

I was puzzled. I thought it was for bananas that we had come to the hills.

'Good heavens!' he said with bitterness. 'To think that you instead of Kenneth should belong to Sandra Street.'

Enchanted Alley

⁂

Leaving for school early on mornings, I walked slowly through the busy parts of the town. The business places would all be opening then and smells of strange fragrance would fill the High Street. Inside the opening doors I would see clerks dusting, arranging, hanging things up, getting ready for the day's business. They looked cheerful and eager and they opened the doors very wide. Sometimes I stood up to watch them.

In places between the stores several little alleys ran off the High Street. Some were busy and some were not and there was one that was long and narrow and dark and very strange. Here, too, the shops would be opening as I passed and there would be bearded Indians in loincloths spreading rugs on the pavement. There would be Indian women also, with veils thrown over their shoulders, setting up their stalls and chatting in a strange sweet tongue. Often I stood, too, watching them, and taking in the fragrance of rugs and spices and onions and sweetmeats. And sometimes, suddenly remembering, I would hurry away for fear the school-bell had gone.

In class, long after I settled down, the thoughts of this alley would return to me. I would recall certain stalls and certain beards and certain flashing eyes, and even some of the rugs that had been rolled out. The Indian women, too, with bracelets around their ankles and around their sun-browned arms flashed to my mind.

I thought of them. I saw them again looking shyly at me from under the shadow of the stores, their veils half hiding their faces. In my mind I could almost picture them laughing together and talking in that strange sweet tongue. And mostly the day would be quite old before the spell of the alley wore off my mind.

One morning I was much too early for school. I passed streetsweepers at work on Harris' Promenade and when I came to the High Street only one or two shop doors were open. I walked slowly, looking at the quietness and noticing some of the alleys that ran away to the backs of fences and walls and distant streets. I looked at the names of these alleys. Some were very funny. And I walked on anxiously so I could look a little longer at the dark, funny street.

As I walked it struck me that I did not know the name of that street. I laughed at myself. Always I had stood there looking along it and I did not know the name of it. As I drew near I kept my eyes on the wall of the corner shop. There was no sign on the wall. On getting there I looked at the other wall. There was a sign-plate upon it but the dust had gathered thickly there and whatever the sign said was hidden behind the dust.

I was disappointed. I looked along the alley which was only now beginning to get alive, and as the shop doors opened the enchantment of spice and onions and sweetmeats emerged. I looked at the wall again but there was nothing there to say what the street was called. Straining my eyes at the sign-plate I could make out a 'c' and an 'A' but farther along the dust had made one smooth surface of the plate and the wall.

'Stupes!' I said in disgust. I heard mild laughter, and as I looked before me I saw the man rolling out his rugs. There were two women beside him and they were talking together and they were laughing and I could see the

20

women were pretending not to look at me. They were setting up a stall of sweetmeats and the man put down his rugs and took out something from a tray and put it into his mouth, looking back at me. Then they talked again in the strange tongue and laughed.

I stood there awhile. I knew they were talking about me. I was not afraid. I wanted to show them that I was not timid and that I would not run away. I moved a step or two nearer the wall. The smells rose up stronger now and they seemed to give the feelings of things splendoured and far away. I pretended I was looking at the wall but I stole glances at the merchants from the corners of my eyes. I watched the men in their loin-cloths and the garments of the women were full and many-coloured and very exciting. The women stole glances at me and smiled to each other and ate of the sweetmeats they sold. The rug merchant spread out his rugs wide on the pavement and he looked at the beauty of their colours and seemed very proud. He, too, looked slyly at me.

I drew a little nearer because I was not afraid of them. There were many more stalls now under the stores. Some of the people turned off the High Street and came into this little alley and they bought little things from the merchants. The merchants held up the bales of cloth and matched them on to the people's clothes and I could see they were saying it looked very nice. I smiled at this and the man with the rugs saw me and smiled.

That made me brave. I thought of the word I knew in the strange tongue and when I remembered it I drew nearer.

'Salaam,' I said.

The rug merchant laughed aloud and the two women laughed aloud and I laughed, too. Then the merchant bowed low to me and replied, 'Salaam!'

This was very amusing for the two women. They talked

21

together so I couldn't understand and then the fat one spoke.

'Wot wrang wid de warl?'

I was puzzled for a moment and then I said, 'Oh, it is the street sign. Dust cover it.'

'Street sign?' one said, and they covered their laughter with their veils.

'I can't read what street it is,' I said, 'What street this is?'

The rug merchant spoke to the women in the strange tongue and the three of them giggled and one of the women said, 'Every marning you stand up dey and you doe know what they carl here?'

'First time I come down here,' I said.

'Yes,' said the fat woman. Her face was big and friendly and she sat squat on the pavement. 'First time you wark down here but every marning you stop dey and watch we.'

I laughed.

'You see 'e laughing?' said the other. The rug merchant did not say anything but he was very much amused.

'What you call this street?' I said. I felt very brave because I knew they were friendly to me, and I looked at the stalls, and the smell of the sweetmeats was delicious. There was barah, too, and chutney and dry channa, and in the square tin there was the wet yellow channa, still hot, the steam curling up from it.

The man took time to put down his rugs and then he spoke to me. 'This,' he said, talking slowly and making actions with his arms, 'From up dey to up dey is Calcatta Street.' He was very pleased with his explanation. He had pointed from the High Street end of the alley to the other end that ran darkly into the distance. The whole street was very long and dusty, and in the concrete drain there was no water and the brown peel of onions blew about when there was a little wind. Sometimes there was the smell of cloves in the air and sometimes the smell of oilcloth, but where I stood the smell of the sweetmeats was strongest and most delicious.

He asked, 'You like Calcatta Street?'

'Yes,' I said.

The two women laughed coyly and looked from one to the other.

'I have to go,' I said,' – school.'

'O you gwine to school?' the man said. He put down his rugs again. His loin-cloth was very tight around him. 'Well you could wark so,' he said, pointing away from the High Street end of the alley, 'and when you get up dey, turn so, and when you wark and wark, you'll meet the school.'

'Oh!' I said, surprised. I didn't know there was a way to school along this alley.

'You see?' he said, very pleased with himself.

'Yes,' I said.

The two women looked at him smiling and they seemed very proud the way he explained. I moved off to go, holding my books under my arm. The women looked at me and they smiled in a sad, friendly way. I looked at the chutney and barah and channa and suddenly something occurred to me. I felt in my pockets and then I opened my books and looked among the pages. I heard one of the women whisper – 'Taking larning. . . .' The other said, 'Aha. . . .' and I did not hear the rest of what she said. Desperately I turned the books down and shook them and the penny fell out rolling on the pavement. I grabbed it up and turned to the fat woman. For a moment I couldn't decide which, but the delicious smell of the yellow, wet channa softened my heart.

'A penny channa,' I said, 'wet.'

The woman bent over with the big spoon, took out a

23

small paper bag, flapped it open, then crammed two or three spoonfuls of channa into it. Then she took up the pepper bottle.

'Pepper?'

'Yes,' I said, anxiously.

'Plenty?'

'Plenty.'

The fat woman laughed, pouring the pepper sauce with two or three pieces of red pepper skin falling on the channa.

'Good!' I said, licking my lips.

'You see?' said the other woman. She grinned widely, her gold teeth glittering in her mouth. 'You see 'e like plenty pepper?'

As I handed my penny I saw the long, brown fingers of the rug merchant stretching over my head. He handed a penny to the fat lady.

'Keep you penny in you pocket,' he grinned at me, 'an look out, you go reach to school late.'

I was very grateful about the penny. I slipped it into my pocket.

'You could wark so,' the man said, pointing up Calcutta Street, 'and turn so, and you'll come down by the school.'

'Yes,' I said, hurrying off.

The street was alive with people now. There were many more merchants with rugs and many more stalls of sweetmeats and other things. I saw bales of bright cloth matched up to ladies' dresses and I heard the ladies laugh and say it was good. I walked fast through the crowd. There were women with sarees calling out 'Ground-nuts! Parata!' and every here and there gramophones blared out Indian songs. I walked on with my heart full inside me. Sometimes I stood up to listen and then I walked on again. Then suddenly it came home to me it must be very late. The crowd was thick and the din spread right along Calcutta Street. I looked back to wave to my friends. They were far behind and the pavement was so crowded I could not see. I heard the car horns tooting and I knew that on the High Street it must be a jam session of traffic and people. It must be very late. I held my books in my hands, secured the paper bag of channa in my pocket, and with the warmth against my legs I ran pell-mell to school.

The Valley of Cocoa

❖❖❖

There was not much in the valley of cocoa. Just the estate and our drying-houses; and our living-house. And the wriggling little river that passed through.

And, of course, the labourers. But they didn't ever seem to speak to anyone. Always they worked silently from sunrise to evening. Only Wills was different. He was friendly, and he knew lots of other things besides things about cocoa and drying-houses.

And he knew Port of Spain. He knew it inside out, he said. Every day after work he would sit down on the log with me and would tell of the wonderful place.

As he spoke his eyes would glow with longing. The longing to be in that world which he said was part of him. And sometimes I knew pain. For Wills had made the city grow in me, and I knew longing, too.

Never had I been out of the valley of cocoa. Father was only concerned about his plantation, and nothing else. He was dedicated to wealth and prosperity, and every year the cocoa yielded more and more. So he grew busier and busier, building, experimenting, planning for record returns. Everything needed out of the valley was handled by Wills – for people who knew Port of Spain could handle anything. Business progressed. The valley grew greener with cocoa, and the drying-houses were so full that the woodmen were always felling timber to build more.

Wills, who one day had just returned from ordering

new machinery in Port of Spain, sat talking with me. The sun had not long gone down but already it was dusk. Wills said it was never so in Port of Spain. Port of Spain was always bright. He said as soon as the sun went down the whole city was lit by electric lamps, and you could hardly tell the difference between night and day. And he explained all about those lamps which he said hung from poles, and from the houses that lined the streets.

It was thick night when we stopped talking and got up. In the darkness Wills walked straight on to a tree, and he swore, and said, By Jove – if that could have happened to him in Port of Spain! He said one of these days I'd go there, when I got big, and I'd see for myself, and I'd never want to come back to the valley again.

The machinery arrived soon afterwards. It came in a shining new van, and the name of the company was spelt in large letters on the sides of the van. The driver was a bright, gay-looking man and when the van stopped he jumped out and laughed and called, 'Hey, there!'

Wills and Father went down to meet him and I eased up behind them. I was thrilled. It was not every day that strangers came to the valley.

Father looked worried as he spoke to the man about payments. He complained that business wasn't doing well and the machinery was so expensive. But the man was laughing all the time, and said who cared about payments when Father had all the time in the world to pay. Father was puzzled, and the man said, yes, Father could pay instalments. Wills said it was true, that's what they did in Port of Spain. The man made Father sign up for instalments and while Father signed, the man pulled at my chin and said, 'Hi!'

Father was paying the first instalment. The man stretched his hands for the money and without counting it he put it into his pocket. Every time my eyes caught his he winked.

'Hi!' he said softly.

I twined round Father's legs.

'Bashful,' he said, 'bashful,' and he tugged at the seat of my pants. I couldn't help laughing.

He opened the door of the van and the next moment he was beside me. He was smiling and dangling a bright coloured packet. I held on to Father's legs. Then I felt something slide into my pocket. I looked up. 'Like sweets?' the man said. I turned away and grinned.

From about my father's legs I watched him. He pulled out a red packet of cigarettes. He passed the cigarettes to Father, then to Wills, and as he lit theirs and lit himself one, he seemed to be taken up with the estate below.

'All yours?' he asked after a while.

Father nodded.

He shook his head approvingly. 'Nice – nice, old man!'

The evening was beginning to darken and the man looked at his watch and said it was getting late and he'd better start burning the gas. Father said true, because Port of Spain was so far, and the country roads were bad enough. The man claimed there were worse roads in some parts of Port of Spain. He laughed and said 'What's a van anyway, only a lot of old iron.' Father and Wills laughed heartily at this, while the man turned a silver key and started the van. Then he said, well cheerio, cheerio, and if anything went wrong with the machine he'd hear from us.

The days that followed were filled with dream. I continually saw the gay city, and the bright, laughing man. Port of Spain, I kept thinking. Port of Spain! I imagined myself among the tall, red houses, the maze of streets, the bright cars and the vans darting to and fro; the trams, the trains, the buses; the thousands of people everywhere. And always I heard the voice. 'Hi!' – it kept sailing back to me. And every time I heard it I smiled.

Months passed, and more and more I grew fed up with the valley. I felt a certain resentment growing inside me. Resentment for everything around. For Father, for the silly labourers; even for Wills. For the cocoa trees. For the hills that imprisoned me night and day. I grew sullen and sick and miserable, tired of it all. I even wished for Father's fears to come true. *Witchbroom!* I wished witchbroom would come and destroy the cocoa and so chase Father from this dreary place.

As expected, the machinery soon went wrong. It wouldn't work. Wills had to rush to Port of Spain to get the man.

I waited anxiously towards the end of that evening, and when in the dusk I saw the van speeding between the trees I nearly jumped from sheer gladness.

From the hill Father shouted saying he didn't know what was wrong but the machine wouldn't start. The man said all right and he boyishly ran up the hill to the house. He stopped and tugged at me and I twined round Father's legs. The man tickled me and we both laughed aloud. Then he gave me sweets in a blue and white packet, and he said he'd better go and see to the machine because the machine was lazy and didn't want to work.

He tried to tickle me again. I jumped away and we laughed, and Father and Wills and he went to the shed. They had not been there five minutes when I heard the machine start again.

The labourers had changed a little. They had become somewhat fascinated by the new machine. It seemed they sometimes stole chances to operate it, for the machine

29

went wrong quite a number of times afterwards. And so, happily, the man often came to us.

In time Father and he became great friends. He gave Father all the hints about cocoa prices in the city and about when to sell and whom to sell to. He knew all the good dealers and all the scamps, he said.

He knew all the latest measures taken to fight cocoa diseases and he told Father what they did in West Africa, and what they did here and what they did there, to fight this, that, and the other disease.

With his help Father did better than ever. And he was so pleased that he asked the man to spend a Sunday with us.

'Sure!' the man agreed. And I ran out then, and made two happy somersaults on the grass.

That Sunday, when the man arrived, I was down the other side of the hill grazing the goats. The voice had boomed down towards me.

'Kenneth!'

I turned and looked round. Then I dropped the ropes and ran excitedly up the hill. 'Coming!' I kept saying, 'Coming!' When I got there the big arms swept me up and threw me up in the air and caught me.

Directly Father called us in to breakfast and afterwards the man put shorts on and we went out into the fresh air. The whole valley of cocoa nestled in the distance below us. The man watched like one under a spell.

'Beautiful!' he whispered, shaking his head. 'Beautiful!'

'And the river,' I said. Strange! I had hardly noticed how pretty the river was.

'Yes,' the man answered. 'Yellow, eh?'

I grinned.

'The water good?'

'Yes,' I said.

'Sure, sure?'

'Sure, sure,' I said.

'Well, come on!' He took me by the hand and we hastened into the house.

The next moment we were running down the hill towards the river, the man in bathing trunks and me with my pants in my hand and sun all over me. We reached the banks and I showed where the water was shallow and where it was deep, and the man plunged into the deep part. He came to the surface again, laughing and saying how nice the water was. He said there was no such river in Port of Spain. He told me to get on his back, and he swam upstream and down with me and then he put me down in the shallow part. Then he soaped my body and bathed me, and when I was rinsed we went and sat a little on the bank.

He sat looking around at the trees and up at the hill. I looked, too, at the view. The cocoa trees seemed greener than I ever remembered seeing them, and the immortelles which stood between the cocoa, for shade, were like great giants, their blooms reddening the sky.

I looked up at him. We smiled.

Quietly, then, he talked of the city. He told me the city was lovely, too, but in a different way. Not like it was here. He said I must see the city one of these days. Everything there was busy. The cars and buses flashed by, and people hurried into the shops, and out of the shops and everywhere. He said he liked the city. It had shops, stores, hotels, hospitals, post offices, schools – everything. Everything that made life easy. But sometimes he grew tired, he said, of the hustle and bustle and nowhere to turn for peace. He said he liked it here, quiet and nice. As life was meant to be. Then his eyes wandered off to the green cocoa again, and the immortelles, and here at the river, and up again to our house on the hill.

And he smiled sadly and said that he wished he was Father to be living here.

We went back into the water for some time. Afterwards the man dried my skin, and his, and we went up to the house.

After we had eaten, Father took us into the cocoa field.

It was quiet there between the trees. The dried brown leaves underfoot, together with the ripening cocoa, put a healthy fragrance in the air.

It was strange being so near those trees. Before I had only known they were there and had watched them from the house, but now I was right in the middle of them, and touching them.

We passed under immortelle trees. The ground beneath the trees was red with dropped flowers and the man picked up the loveliest of the flowers and gave them to me. Father broke a cocoa pod, and we sucked the seeds and juicy pulp, and really, the young cocoa was as sweet as Wills had told me. The man sucked his seeds dry and looked as if he wanted more, so I laughed. And Father, watching from the corner of his eyes, understood, and said, 'Let's look for a nice ripe cocoa.'

It was already evening when we took the path out. Father and the young man were talking and I heard Father ask him what he thought of the place.

'Great, Mr Browne,' he answered. 'Mr Browne, it's great, I'm telling you!'

Later, late that night I eased up from the bed. I unlatched the window and quietly shifted the curtain from one side.

The valley lay quietly below. The cocoa leaves seemed to be playing with the moonlight and the immortelles stood there, looking tall and lonely and rapt in peace.

From the shadows the moonlight spread right across the river and up the hill.

'Beautiful. . . !' the voice sailed back to my mind. And I wondered where he was now, if he was already in Port of Spain. He had been sorry to leave. He had said this was one of the happiest days he had known. I had heard him telling Father how he liked the valley so much and how much he liked the little boy. I had cried then.

And now it swept back to my mind – what he had told Father just as he was leaving. He had said, 'Mr Browne, don't be afraid for witchbroom. Not a thing will happen. Just you use that spray – you know – and everything will be all right.'

Quickly then I drew the curtains and latched the window. And I squeezed the pillow to me, for joy.

The Patch of Guava

❖❖❖

The path was still there. Although it was overlaid with nettles and minnie-root, and long razor-grass, no big trees had sprung up on it. It had kept very well with the years, save that on either side the bigger trees had arched in upon it, forming a thick canopy above.

Mr Johnson, being a tall man, had to bend a little to walk through the canopy. He walked with a half-smile of intense surprise on his face. When he got out into the clear again and he looked out upon the low ground before him he smiled broadly in wonderment. And he trembled just a little. The field of guava was still there. Yes, still there after these many, many years.

For a while he looked about him. There were the familiar coconut trees around and a squirrel branched from one tree to the other. Mr Johnson looked at this. It was the same with these trees, too; even with the squirrels it was the same.

Now he continued down the path towards a cluster of coconut trees. For a moment he stopped to play his hands in the stream that ran nearby. The stream ran so swiftly now, it was as though it had become sprightlier with the years. The elderly man was struck by this as he went on.

On reaching the coconut clump it was not difficult to find the tree he had been thinking of. He went up to examine the bark, and then he could hardly believe his eyes. Yes, the mark 'EC' was still there. He could not remember what had happened to the penknife that carved it, nor did he know what had become of Emmy. But the 'EC' he had notched out as a child could still be seen.

Mr Johnson put his hands to his grey hairs. He could hear his heart thumping as he walked on and into the field of guava that sprawled before him.

It being the dry season, the dead guava leaves had fallen thickly, forming a crisp, brown carpet underfoot. There was yellow fruit between the branches but beneath the trees themselves there was no growth, and the green leaves kept out the sun. The trees stood in the same jaunty fashion as they had stood in the far-off days.

Mr Johnson walked right on, slowly, and still in wonderment, until he came to the lily pond. As usual, it was covered with lilies, some withered, some with their flowers folded in the heat of the day.

The old man sat down on the dead leaves at the edge of the pond. This was the pond where they had come to fetch water in the dry season. He, Emmy, Molly, Kitsin, and Coots. What about those children? – he thought – those East Indian neighbours he used to have? And then he chuckled. Those children would not be children any more. But he had heard nothing of them except that they had gone away.

He felt a profound longing inside of him. They had been so much a part of himself. All his childhood days were filled with them. But they were gone now. Gone long ago and gone forever. And if they were still on this side of the grave they would be old and feeble like himself.

At last he got up, rather laboriously. He brushed his seat with his hands and he turned back the way he had come. As he drew out of the guava patch he picked handfuls and handfuls of guava and crammed his pockets with them.

Time had indeed lain a light hand on the village. Some of the old people had died, and the middle-aged ones had filled their places. And new, young ones had replaced the middle-aged. Most of the youths had gone away. Some old houses had been demolished and there were a few new ones. The Post Office had been shifted to the middle of the village, and an aged, imposing pomme-cythere tree on the hill had disappeared from the scene. But apart from that the place had not altered much.

For Mr Johnson it was easy to settle down again in this village of his youth. In fact, to a great extent it was as though he had never gone away. In spite of all his years in other parts, here was where he belonged and here was where he felt at home. The old family house had been left to him and he at first had been reluctant to come back. But now he was excited and he was determined to transform the property into a place to live in.

And now the little garden behind the house was a sight to admire. The corn had grown tall among the ochroes and melongenes, and the redness of ripening tomatoes met the eye. There was also a great deal of cassava and pigeon peas and yams, and as he was a man who liked fruit, there were little plum and portugal trees bursting out around the house.

The villagers marvelled. Mr Johnson had not long come among them and already there was such a change over the abandoned place. Apart from the garden, the old house had been repaired and repainted and they felt that the vigour of this man was an inspiration to them all.

In a quick time the whole village began to look upon him as an example.

It was hardly a year following Mr Johnson's return that a few men with briefcases began passing down the path.

They appeared to be businessmen. They asked Mr Johnson's permission and they walked right down to the area behind the house.

Mr Johnson was a little puzzled, but not worried. He was not even very curious. He only wondered what such well-groomed men wanted in those bushes. Soon he hardly noticed them until one day one of the briefcase men met him in the path. 'Hello,' the man cried, and stopped to talk. And he explained what their business was.

' – Yes,' the briefcase man went on, 'we'll be producing all kinds of things here, Mr . . . what's the name?'

'Johnson.'

'We'll be producing all kinds of things here, Mr Johnson. You can't imagine. All sorts of things – cocoa and chocolate products, coconut and copra and coconut-oil, oatmeal, oil-cake, mattress fibre . . .' and he paused as if even he were amazed at the extent of the undertaking.

Mr Johnson stared at him. Then he looked at the ground about him as though he had lost his words there. Instead of speaking he sighed. Then he said, 'I – I think we here like the place as it is. I think we prefer to live in quietness and peace.'

'Quietness and peace!' the businessman exclaimed. 'Good heavens! hear this man. Think of what a factory would do to this area, Mr Johnson. Think of what it would mean to this backward place. Think of the people – the hundreds that would be employed with us. Think of progress, Mr Johnson, *progress*. There never was such a development in this area before.'

Mr Johnson thought: 'Thank God for that.' But he did not say anything. He stood there, almost wistfully, looking at the businessman. He was feeling powerless. The businessman, having given expression to his feelings, looked about him, contemplating the lie of the land. He had the whole building project vividly in his head, and as he looked he could almost see the factories sprawled out in front of him, their chimneys puffing smoke, the mills grinding. He could almost hear the hum of industry break out over the silent place.

He turned around to Mr Johnson. His satisfaction was more than he could contain. He said, 'Look at that lovely flat place! A real beauty. The only work we have to do is to get rid of that guava patch.'

'But why?' Mr Johnson said, 'But why? But why the guava patch?'

The businessman could hardly believe his ears and swung round to Mr Johnson. 'You want it to remain there?' he cried hastily. The veins stuck out in his neck. 'You want malaria, typhoid; that's what you want? Listen, Mr Johnson,' he said, 'It's no good being the sentimental, poetry type. This world is blood and sweat and pressure, not poetry.' And he stormed off down the path.

Mr Johnson stood there and watched him go. Then he looked at the guava patch, and what with the distress inside him, the memories of other years flooded his mind. He could not help escaping from the world about him and being a boy again in this same guava patch with Emmy, Molly, Kitsin and Coots. He could not help being a child, wild and free and as supple as the guava limbs themselves. His thoughts were in those days for a while and then they came back to the businessman, and it was as though he were hearing the booming voice again: 'You want malaria, typhoid. . . . This world is pressure not poetry!'

He looked around. No one was there. He said aloud, 'It's you fellers who giving the pressure. You can't see anything unless you want to spoil it. You people messing up this place.' His heart pained him. He knew that when

38

the briefcase men started work the village would never be the same again.

There and then a thought struck him and he turned back along the path towards the coconut trees. He soon came upon the businessman.

He said, 'Chief, when you all going to start up?'

The businessman was taken aback and pleasantly surprised. He beamed. 'Well,' he said, 'We are almost ready, Mr Johnson. Let's see. Tuesday we should begin the cutting down and levelling, and say by the beginning of the month the material should be here already and the construction should really get going.'

'Okay. Good, eh? Thanks,' Mr Johnson said. And he went back up the path.

The people who were to build the great factory complex were people with little time to waste. For sure enough Tuesday morning dawned on the labour of workmen in the area behind the house. They had started on the guava patch. Chop! Chop! Chop! the cutlasses went. Chop! Chop! Chop! And the guava trees moaned and fell.

The businessman was standing on the high ground and looking at the work. But suddenly the plans in his briefcase flashed to his mind and he turned around. He had brought those plans expressly to show Mr Johnson. Anxiously he went through the arch of trees.

When he reached the house he shouted, almost bellowed, Mr Johnson's name. The neighbour next door heard and hurried over to meet him. She said, 'Sir, Mr Johnson not there, you know. I don't know what happen – everybody so surprised. Last year he came back here suddenly, and everybody thought he was happy. But yesterday he just pack up and gone just like that.'

Cricket in the Road

✣✣✣

In the rainy season we got few chances to play cricket in the road. For whenever we were at the game, the rains came down, chasing us into the yard again. That was the way it was in Mayaro in the rainy season. The skies were always overcast, and over the sea the rainclouds hung low and grey and scowling, and the winds blew in and whipped angrily through the palms. And when the winds were strongest and raging, the low-hanging clouds would become dense and black, and the sea would roar, and the torrents of rain would come sweeping with all their tumult upon us.

We had just run in from the rain. Amy and Vern from next door were in good spirits, and laughing for oddly enough they seemed to enjoy the downpour as much as playing cricket in the road. Amy was in our yard, giggling and pretending to drink the falling rain, with her face all wet and her clothes drenched, and Vern who was sheltering under the eaves, excitedly jumped out to join her. 'Rain, rain, go to Spain,' they shouted. And presently their mother, who must have heard the noise and knew, appeared from next door, and Vern and Amy vanished through the hedge.

I stood there, depressed about the rain, and then I put Vern's bat and ball underneath the house, and went indoors. 'Stupes!' I said to myself. I had been batting when the rains came down. It was only when *I* was batting that the rains came down! I wiped my feet so

40

I wouldn't soil the sheets, and went up on the bed. I was sitting, sad, and wishing that the rain would really go away – go to Spain, as Vern said – when my heart seemed to jump out of me. A deafening peal of thunder struck across the sky.

Quickly I closed the window. The rain hammered awfully on the roof-top and I kept tense for the thunder which I knew would break again and for the unearthly flashes of lightning.

Secretly I was afraid of the violent weather. I was afraid of the rain, and of the thunder and the lightning that came with them, and of the sea beating against the headlands, and of the storm-winds, and of everything being so death-like when the rains were gone. I started again at another flash of lightning and before I had recovered from this, yet another terrifying peal of thunder hit the air. I screamed. I heard my mother running into the room. Thunder struck again and I dashed under the bed.

'Selo! Selo! First bat!' Vern shouted from the road. The rains had ceased and the sun had come out, but I was not quite recovered yet. I brought myself reluctantly to look out from the front door, and there was Vern, grinning and impatient and beckoning to me.

'First bat,' he said. And as if noting my indifference he looked towards Amy who was just coming out to play. 'Who second bat?' he said.

'Me!' I said.

'Me!' shouted Amy almost at the same time.

'Amy second bat,' Vern said.

'No, I said "Me" first,' I protested.

Vern grew impatient while Amy and I argued. Then an idea seemed to strike him. He took out a penny from his pocket. 'Toss for it,' he said. 'What you want?'

41

'Heads,' I called.

'Tail,' cried Amy, 'Tail bound to come!'

The coin went up in the air, fell down and overturned, showing tail.

'I'm *not* playing!' I cried, stung. And as that did not seem to disturb enough, I ran towards where I had put Vern's bat and ball and disappeared with them behind our house. Then I flung them with all my strength into the bushes.

When I came back to the front of the house, Vern was standing there dumbfounded. 'Selo, where's the bat and ball,' he said.

I was fuming. 'I don't know about *any* bat and ball!'

'Tell on him,' Amy cried. 'He throw them away.'

Vern's mouth twisted into a forced smile. 'What's an old bat and ball,' he said.

But as he walked out of the yard I saw tears glinting from the corners of his eyes.

For the rest of that rainy season we never played cricket in the road again. Sometimes the rains ceased and the sun came out brightly, and I heard the voices of Amy and Vern on the other side of the fence. At such times I would go out into the road and whistle to myself, hoping they would hear me and come out, but they never did, and I knew they were still very angry and would never forgive me.

And so the rainy season went on. And it was as fearful as ever with the thunder and lightning and waves roaring in the bay, and the strong winds. But the people who talked of all this said that was the way Mayaro was, and they laughed about it. And sometimes when through the rain and even thunder I heard Vern's voice on the other side of the fence, shouting 'Rain, rain, go to Spain,' it puzzled me how it could be so. For often I had made up

42

my mind I would be brave, but when the thunder cracked I always dashed under the bed.

It was the beginning of the new year when I saw Vern and Amy again. The rainy season was, happily, long past, and the day was hot and bright and as I walked towards home I saw that I was walking towards Vern and Amy just about to start cricket in the road. My heart thumped violently. They looked strange and new as if they had gone away, far, and did not want to come back any more. They did not notice me until I came up quite near, and then I saw Amy start, her face all lit up.

'Vern –' she cried, 'Vern look – look Selo!'

Embarrassed, I looked at the ground and at the trees, and at the orange sky, and I was so happy I did not know what to say. Vern stared at me, a strange grin on his face. He was ripping the celophane paper off a brand new bat.

'Selo, here – *you* first bat,' he said gleefully.

And I cried as though it were raining and I was afraid.

Hibiscus

✤✤✤

'Aren't you excited?' my aunt asked. Although she smiled, her face looked a bit drawn, and I knew the situation had more effect on her than on me.

'Yes,' I said.

'I'll buy up everything,' she said. 'You shouldn't need too much clothes. You should reach there by Easter.'

I didn't say anything. I didn't particularly want to talk. I didn't care if I reached there by Easter. I lay, looking at the ceiling, looking at my aunt sometimes, sometimes looking at the nurses walking through the wards.

'They can't keep you, you know!' said my aunt.

'No,' I said.

'You want to go?'

'If you don't want me to. . . .'

'No, you must go; it's good for you. The sunshine is good.'

'All right.'

'You're looking much better today.'

I told her what they were giving me now.

'Oh, good!' she said.

I never forgot to tell her what they were giving me. She always wanted to know. She was very impressed with what they had been giving me. My pneumonia was almost gone in a matter of just three weeks.

She glanced at the clock. It was drawing near the end of visiting time. She began taking out the little things she had brought me. She rested the handbag on the bed. With each item she watched to see if I was glad.

Bananas, sweets, orange juice, grapes. She put them on the locker. I was fed up with sweets for one thing. Bananas I enjoyed sometimes. I wanted to be glad but I was feeling too weak to try. Auntie paused.

'You like blackcurrant juice.'

'Don't bring any blackcurrant juice.'

'I brought a little bottle,' she said entreatingly.

I didn't like blackcurrant juice. She looked down at me. 'It's good,' she said.

'Don't bring any more,' I said.

She took out a few more things and I lay there not paying any mind at all. My thoughts just seemed to be going round and round. Really, she could have put anything on the locker and I wouldn't have cared once she didn't ask me if I liked it.

'Brought you something to read,' she said, probing deep in the handbag. She took the book out, and I saw it was a little soft-cover book with the picture of a flower on the cover. 'West Indian stories,' she said.

That brightened me a little. I turned on my side and took the book in my hands.

She beamed: 'You didn't think they'd have West Indian books here, eh?'

'No,' I said.

'Well you have something to occupy yourself with. Don't read too much though.'

'No, Auntie.'

It was the end of visiting time. The bell was ringing and visitors were trickling out. Auntie got up. 'I'll write and tell them when you'll be sailing. All depends on Doctor. What boat you came up on, again?'

'*Hildebrand.*'

She bent down to me. 'It might be the *Hildebrand* again,' she encouraged.

She squeezed my hand and she left. 'See you tomorrow evening,' she stopped at the door to call back.

As usual, it was only when Auntie left that I thought of her a little. I didn't think a lot now because I didn't feel that way in the atmosphere of drugs and needles; but at times I knew how good Auntie was to me. I had always been her favourite at home. As soon as she came to England it was me she sent for. Now I was sick and with Doctor's advice she was sending me home for two months. Then, too, she came to see me every day. She brought the bananas and sweets and oranges faster than I could make presents of them.

I looked at the book she brought. Of course I recognized the flower on the cover. I smiled. The book title was printed in large, black letters at the top: HIBISCUS AND OTHER STORIES. I looked down at the bottom. BY C. C. MATTHEWS. I studied the flower again. It was a perfect likeness. We had hibiscus all over Trinidad. Especially in Mayaro. No one paid any mind to hibiscus. Except, of course, C. C. Matthews. C. C. Matthews had written a story about it.

I opened to the first page. It said the book was FOR MARIANA. There was a little Latin quotation. Perhaps Mariana was studying Latin, I thought. There were people who studied that; I hated blackcurrant juice only a little less than I hated Latin.

I turned again and there was the index. I read down the list.

Hibiscus
The Way of the Hot Sun
The Balata Tree
Come Back to the Islands
Beneath the Tropic Stars
Carib Love-Spear

I counted. Six. Six stories, then by C. C. Matthews. I closed the book and looked at the hibiscus picture again. It was really a wonderful job. It seemed as if C. C. Matthews had taken a moment off from beneath the tropic stars to paint the flower himself. He must have done it under the Balata tree, reddening it with rich, thick blood from his Carib love-spear.

The nurse was making the rounds with the thermo-meters. I rested the book down. I was surprised to find what my imagination was doing with the story titles. I noticed that my hands shook a little. The nurse came, put the thermometer into my mouth, and took the book up casually.

'Reading this?' she said.

'Yes,' I replied, embarrassed. This was the nurse who had said funny things to me.

'Look at this little boy,' she said, 'reading about love.'

'No,' I said.

'You're telling me! They're all packed with love.'

'No,' I said.

She was smiling wickedly. Her eyes were large and black and they looked very mischievous. She turned pages. 'Oh, yes!' she half exclaimed, 'Carib love-spear! Aye, aye!'

I felt stung with guilt. I tried to explain but the nurse put a finger to her lips and said I was not to talk with the thermometer in my mouth. Then she looked at her watch and took the thermometer out, looking at my reaction all the time. 'Whoops!' she cried, watching the reading. Then she bent down to me. 'I say, you'll lend me that book, will you?'

I sunk my head in my pillow and laughed so she wouldn't see me.

When all was quiet again and the nurse went off duty

I settled down to read HIBISCUS AND OTHER STORIES. I was surprised when on reading 'Hibiscus' itself I discovered that the scene was set in Mayaro, my own village. The story told of a little girl who, on going for water in Spring Flat, sung gaily to the hibiscus who were her friends. They loved her because she sang to them and no one else took notice of them. And in her song she told them how very pretty they were. This made them redder than usual because they were embarrassed, though glad, and when the hummingbirds came for the nectar they kept, they told the hummingbirds what the little girl sang. They asked the hummingbirds as reward for the nectar to show their friend where the water was purest and clear. And they promised the little girl that in her afterlife they would make her into a large, red hibiscus and she would sing among them.

This story touched me very keenly, for I had known Spring Flat and had known the hibiscus road that led to the springs. The way C. C. Matthews wrote about it made me certain he had lived at Mayaro and had known that place, too. And I tried to think if I had ever known any Matthews at all or any Mariana. For, indeed, Mariana must have been real. Mariana must have walked past our house with her little bucket going down to the springs. I must have even heard her sing and cannot now remember. I must have even spoken to C. C. Matthews about the red hibiscus, and the hibiscus must have turned redder for hearing us!

I read 'Hibiscus' once more and feeling in a happy spirit I read the other stories. They were all beautifully written and there was something whimsical about them. 'Beneath the Tropic Stars' gave a peculiar sensation of twinkling lights and pitch-black sky, and palms whispering along surf-kissed shores, and when after reading this I read 'Come Back to the Islands', it seemed as if all these things were calling to me. I am coming, I thought, being too weak to resist, and I felt that when Auntie came I would tell her I was glad to go and I was excited. But when I read 'Carib Love-Spear' I was genuinely excited and ashamed because I had read about love.

I went through the book but 'Hibiscus' was the story which was now one with my mind and making circles with it. I thought of Mariana and C. C. Matthews and was glad to be going home again across the sea. I wondered if Mariana had ever crossed the sea. Perhaps. Perhaps that was why C. C. Matthews had written 'Come Back to the Islands'. Light seemed to spread across my mind. I was anxious for Auntie to come. For I was sure somehow that she would remember someone in Mayaro by name of Matthews and maybe a little girl, Mariana.

It turned out that Auntie wasn't sure she knew any Matthews. Maybe. Mariana? Maybe. Maybe Auntie knew everybody in Mayaro. But four years was enough time to forget. Auntie wouldn't commit herself. She couldn't say for certain.

What she could say was that she had heard from home again. They were expecting me. They were all very jubilant that I would be coming home for two months. They promised that they wouldn't keep me but that they'd let me come back. Auntie had made sure about that. She had shown me the return ticket.

She had spoken to the doctor, too, and they had fixed a date. Feeling so much better now, I realized that I was looking forward to the long sea journey. This was strange, for since the pneumonia I hadn't looked forward to anything. Now I thought all the time of rolling sea, then land again, and me walking home along the hibiscus road.

I thought of my parents only a little. I had never missed

49

them much. I hadn't had a chance to miss them, being with Auntie. When Auntie loved you she didn't let you miss anybody, the way she treated you. As for the sunshine, I didn't think about that before until I read 'Come Back to the Islands'. Then it was that I recalled the warmth of the sun on my skin and the freshness of the Island breeze. And what with the goodness of the drugs and the good tonic of HIBISCUS AND OTHER STORIES, I felt keen and fit when the day for my journey arrived.

In the Islands Easter came, and Easter, also, was the time of the hibiscus. Every week I wrote to Auntie. There was a Post Office along the hibiscus road, and every time I went in to buy air letters I wrote, 'Dear Auntie, How I wish you were here!' In the village there was a lot of change. There were new shops and houses rising up all around, and the tar was still fresh on the electricity poles. Station Hill was cut down, and they were going to build a new Government School and move the old one to Plaisance. But Change had stayed there and had not walked along the hibiscus road. Nor had it been to the springs. The Flats were green with sage and there were the fresh, clean pools, the best water being where the hibiscus flowers were reddest. And when I saw the sun shine as it did I knew here there would be no pneumonia or anything like it, and I wondered if C. C. Matthews had written about pneumonia.

And so I was happy about coming back to the Islands though I was very sad about not hearing of C. C. Matthews. No one I asked had ever heard about him. When I said he was a writer who wrote books they laughed and said no writer would live in Mayaro. They asked me where I had heard about him and I said England. They looked at me and asked if I had been in England. I swore to it and when I made them believe me they said that C. C. Matthews was probably in England because English people liked to write books. That made me despair. English people were not the only people who wrote books. And C. C. Matthews couldn't be an Englishman and write about hibiscus. So although I was happy for the sun and the warm, strange nights, yet I was unhappy. No one knew C. C. Matthews and very few remembered me at all. I walked down the road to the springs and there was no little girl singing to the hibiscus, and the hummingbirds that fluttered about for the nectar went nowhere near the shining pools. And when I went to buy air-letters I wrote, 'Dear Auntie, I have already been here six weeks, and I am glad that I am coming back to you.'

It was now only a matter of days for my return. My parents were excited about me. My friends were excited, too, about my returning to England. And I thought of the good time I could have had if only I could be sure of C. C. Matthews and Mariana. Or if I had not known about them at all. And so one evening I left the house sadly and walked down the hibiscus road and when I saw an old man coming home with the cows I stopped and spoke to him.

'Matthews?' he said, and he meditated a little and seemed to turn the word over on his tongue.

'He used to write,' I said, hopefully.

'He used to write, eh,' the man said. I could see that his thoughts travelled far into memory. 'I know one Matthews who used to be sexton.'

'No,' I said, 'that wouldn't be him. He wrote about. . . .' And feeling embarrassed to say he wrote about love, I halted.

'What?' the man said, 'What did he write about?'

There was anxiety in his eyes, and a shaking of his

fingers, and I knew I couldn't deceive the old man.

'He wrote about love,' I said, turning my eyes to the grass.

'And what about love?' he asked.

I did not answer.

'What's your name?' he said.

'Roy.'

'Well, Roy,' he said, 'Everything is love, life is love, *God* is love.'

The place was completely still so that I could hear the cows munching the grass, and I could hear the chains jingle when they moved a step or two.

'This Mr Matthews,' I said, 'No one seems to know him.'

'I think . . .' said the old man reflectively, 'I think they call him by another name.'

'Perhaps that's not the man,' I said. 'I believe there was a girl, a little girl. . . .'

'Mariana?' asked the old man.

I was stunned. 'Yes,' I cried, 'that is the man! You know Mariana?'

'I used to,' he said. 'I wouldn't any more now, though. She went to study in England. He missed her so much. He wrote for her to come back. She wouldn't come back any more now.'

'Why?' I cried, my heart feeling heavy. I watched his face. Despair, like a raging storm, seemed breaking over him.

'You wouldn't understand,' he said. 'You – you are a little boy. You wouldn't understand what pneumonia is.'

And I, too, wilted. I felt faint and weak. I didn't answer, and it was true I was a little boy, but heaven knew I understood. I saw clearly now why Mariana wouldn't come back and why the old man was crying for her. I remembered *Come Back to the Islands*, and

I realized his was a sickness no amount of drugs could cure. I felt giddy and faint and as if the fevers were coming on again. I turned around to see if there was any hibiscus flower redder than all the rest.

And then weakly I turned back to the old man. He looked away. 'I'm not crying,' he said. 'It's only so sometimes.' He seemed to be having great difficulty speaking. And then he said again, 'I'm not crying. But a little writing isn't anything really. But if you have a little one and it's the only one – well it's a hell of a thing.'

Drunkard of the River

✤✤✤

'Where you' father?'

The boy did not answer. He paddled his boat carefully between the shallows, and then he ran the boat alongside the bank, putting his paddle in front to stop it. Then he threw the rope round the picket and helped himself on to the bank. His mother stood in front of the door still staring at him.

'Where you' father?'

The boy hid his anger. He looked at his mother and said calmly, 'You know Pa. You know where he is.'

'And ah did tell you not to come back without 'im?'

'I could bring Pa back?' the boy cried. His bitterness was getting the better of him. 'When Pa went to drink I could bring him back? How?'

It was always the same. The boy's mother stood in front of the door staring up the river. Every Saturday night it was like this. Every Saturday night Mano went out to the village and drank himself helpless and lay on the floor of the shop, cursing and vomiting until the Chinaman was ready to close up. Then they rolled Mano outside and heaven knows, maybe they even spat on him.

The boy's mother stared up the river, her face twisted with anger and distress. She couldn't go up the river now. It would be fire and brimstone if she went. But Mano had to be brought home. She turned to see what the boy was doing. He had packed away the things from the shopping bag and he was now reclining on the couch.

'You have to go for you' father, you know,' she said.

'Who?'

'You!'

'Not me!'

'Who you tellin' not me,' she shouted. She was furious now. 'Dammit, you have to go for you' father!'

Sona had risen from the couch on the alert. His mother hardly ever hit him now but he could never tell. It had been a long time since she had looked so angry and had stamped her feet.

He rose slowly and reluctantly and as he glanced at her he couldn't understand what was wrong with her. He couldn't see why she bothered about his father at all. For his father was stupid and worthless and made their life miserable. If he could have had his way, Mano would have been out of the house a long time now. His bed would have been the dirty meat-table in front of Assing's shop. That was what he deserved. The rascal! The boy spat through the window. The very thought of his father sickened him.

Yet with Sona's mother it was different. The man she had married and who had turned out badly was still the pillar of her life. Although he had piled up grief after grief, tear after tear, she felt lost and drifting without him. To her he was as mighty as the very river that flowed outside. She remembered that in his young days there was nothing any living man could do that he could not.

In her eyes he was still young. He did not grow old. It was she who had aged. He had only turned out badly. She hated him for the way he drank rum and squandered the little money he worked for. But she did not mind the money so much. It was seeing him drunk. She knew when he staggered back how she would shake with rage

55

and curse him, but even so, how inside she would shake
with the joy of having him safe and home.

She wondered what was going on at the shop now.
She wondered if he was already drunk and helpless and
making a fool of himself.

With Sona, the drunkard's son, this was what stung
more than ever. The way Mano, his father, cursed everybody and made a fool of himself. Sometimes he had
listened to his father and he had wanted to kick him
because he was so ashamed. Often in silence he had
shaken his fist and said, 'One day, ah'll – ah'll. . . .'

He had watched his mother put up with sweat and
starvation. She was getting skinnier every day, and she
looked more like fifty-six than the thirty-six she was.
Already her hair was greying. Sometimes he had looked
at her and, thinking of his father, he had ground his
teeth and had said, 'Beast!' several times to himself. He
was in that frame of mind now. Bitter and reluctant, he
went to untie the boat.

'If I can't bring 'im, I'll leave 'im,' he said angrily.

'Get somebody to help you!'

He turned to her. 'Nobody wouldn't help me. He insult
everybody. Last week Bolai kick 'im.'

'Bolai kick 'im? An' what you do?'

His mother was stung with rage and shock. Her eyes
were large and red and watery.

The boy casually unwound the rope from the picket.
'What I do?' he said. 'That is he and Bolai business.'

His mother burst out crying.

'What ah must do?' the boy said. 'All the time ah
say, "Pa, come home, come home, Pa!" You know what
he tell me? He say, "Go to hell, yuh little bastard!"'

His mother turned to him. Beads of tears were still
streaming down the sides of her face.

'Sona, go for you' father. Go now. You stand up there

56

and watch Bolai kick you' father and you ain't do nothing? He mind you, you know,' she sobbed. 'He is you' father, you ungrateful. . . .' And choking with anger and grief she burst out crying again.

When she raised her head, Sona was paddling towards midstream, scowling, avoiding the shallows of the river.

True enough there was trouble in Assing's shop. Mano's routine was well under way. He staggered about the bar dribbling and cursing.

Again and again, the Chinaman spoke to him about his words. Not that he cared about Mano's behaviour. The rum Mano consumed made quite a difference to Assing's account. It safeguarded Mano's freedom of speech in the shop.

But the customers were disgusted. All sorts of things had happened on Saturday nights through Mano's drunkenness. There was no such thing as buying in peace once Mano was there.

So now with trouble looming, the arrival of Sona was sweet relief. As Sona walked in, someone pointed out his father between the sugar bags.

'Pa!'

Mano looked up. 'What you come for?' he drawled.

'Ma say to come home,' Sona said. He told himself that he mustn't lose control in front of strangers.

'Well!'

'Ma send me for you.'

'You! You' mother send you for me! So you is me father now, eh – eh?' In his drunken rage the old man staggered towards his son.

Sona didn't walk back. He never did anything that would make him feel stupid in front of a crowd. But before he realized what was happening his father lunged forward and struck him a blow across his face.

57

'So you is me father, eh? You is me father, now!' He cried, and threw a kick at the boy.

Two or three people bore down on Mano and held him off the boy. Sona put his hands to his belly where his father had just kicked him. Tears came to his eyes. The drunkenness was gripping Mano more and more. He could hardly stand by himself now. He was struggling to set himself free. The men held on to him. Sona kept out of the way.

'It's a damn' shame!' somebody shouted.

'Shame?' Mano drawled. 'An' he is me father now, 'e modder send him for me. Let me go,' he cried, struggling more than ever. 'I'll kill 'im. So help me God, I'll kill 'im!'

They hadn't much to do to control Mano in this state. His body was loose and weak now, his bones seemed to be turning to water. The person who had cried, 'It's a damn' shame!' spoke again.

'Why you don't carry 'im home, boy? You can't see he only making trouble?'

'You'll help me put 'im in the boat?' Sona asked. He looked calm now. He seemed only concerned with getting his father out of the shop, and out of all this confusion. Nobody could tell what went on below the calmness of his face. Nobody could guess that hate was blazing in his mind.

Four men and Sona lifted Mano and carted him into the boat. Sona pushed off. After a while he looked back at the bridge. Everything behind was swallowed by the darkness. 'Pa,' the boy said. His father groaned. 'Pa, yuh going home,' Sona said.

The wilderness of mangroves and river spread out before the boat. They were alone. Sona was alone with Mano, and the river and the mangroves and the night, and the swarms of alligators below. He looked at his

58

father again. 'Pa, so you kick me up then, eh?' he said.

Far into the night Sona's mother waited. She slept a little on one side, then she turned on the other side, and at every sound she woke up, straining her ears. There was no sound of the paddle on water. Surely the shops must have closed by now, she thought. Everything must have closed by this time. She lay anxious and listened until her eyes shut again in an uneasy sleep.

She was awakened by the creaking of the bedroom floor. Sona jumped back when she spoke.

'Who that – Mano?'

'Is me, Ma,' Sona said.

His bones, too, seemed to be turning liquid. Not from drunkenness, but from fear. The lion in him had changed into a lamb. As he spoke his voice trembled.

His mother didn't notice. 'All you now come?' she said. 'Where Mano?'

The boy didn't answer. In the darkness he took down his things from the nail-pegs.

'Where Mano?' his mother cried out.

'He out there sleeping. He drunk.'

'The monster,' his mother said, getting up and feeling for the matches.

Sona quickly slipped outside. Fear dazed him now and he felt dizzy. He looked at the river and he looked back at the house and there was only one word that kept hitting against his mind: Police! Police! He knew what would happen. He felt desperate.

'Mano!' he heard his mother call to the emptiness of the house, 'Mano!'

Panic-stricken, Sona fled into the mangroves and into the night.

The Day of the Fearless

✻✻✻

The train raced in at sundown. It hustled forward maddeningly along the rails, and, when it got to North Bend, it seemed to scream as it hugged the curving yard lines. And after the North Bend there was the town a little way in the distance. The train seemed to run on the very edge of the sea wall and on the other side, the rows of railway buildings and repair yards and old locomotives whizzed by.

Then the train gave a loud whistle as it passed the signalbox and after that there were a few jerks and the carriages began slowing down.

Passengers put their heads out of the window to look at the town. Some of them had only left San Fernando that morning. Some had been away for weeks. Willis held the brown paper parcel under his arm and stared at the railway station and at the red houses that stretched away to the hills. Then he walked stiffly to the other side of the train and looked at the jetty and at the motor-launches out in the gulf. He had not seen San Fernando for two years.

The carriages made bigger jerks now and the rows of railway buildings and old locomotives passed by more slowly. Presently they entered the great arch of the railway station and came to the platforms with the train crawling to a stop. Willis watched the crowds on the platform and shrunk back a little. It was the same sort of crowd that had lined the platform when he was taken

60

away. On that occasion he had been hustled between two policemen and put quickly into the small cross-barred compartment. But the crowd had still seen him and had raised their voices and had used insulting words. And he had even been as hostile as the crowd and turned to shout back. But the policemen had pushed him forward with a truncheon against the small of his back.

Now he pulled his hat right down over his eyes. He was not hostile but ashamed and a little afraid. Two years was a long time. He was not thinking of the soreness of his body. Because whether you were meek or difficult, it made no difference to the warders. One just had no right to be behind bars. That was the warders' reasoning. Maybe they were right. He was a little afraid because he didn't want to be behind bars any more. He hoped they would leave him alone now. In a town, once you lived meekly no one troubled you. But once the gang knew you they did not leave you alone. It didn't matter whether you had changed or not. They didn't realize two years was a long time to think. And although the other people never troubled you, they kept away from you and walked on the other side of the street when they heard you had spent two years in jail for wounding. It didn't matter to them whether you were a new man or not.

The carriages clanged against each other and jerked to a stop. The crowd was thick on the platform. Willis pulled his hat deeper over his eyes and his mind was really troubled. He wasn't sure that he should have come back to this town.

As Willis stepped out onto the wharf he gazed about him like a child. Two years had made quite a difference to San Fernando. The town seemed more open, more outspread. Everything, in fact, looked bigger and more outspread. Maybe it was because the world had suddenly broken loose from the limits of a six foot by six foot cell!

The fear in Willis' heart had died down. He had walked through the crowd on the platform and onto the wharf and no one had taken any notice of him. No one whispered to the other and said 'look. . . .' He had watched their mouths and their eyes but none took notice of him. They had forgotten about him. Perhaps some knew. And perhaps they pretended to forget because they had forgiven.

Maybe he would be able to settle down and live in peace. Maybe. . . . And then he thought of the gang. They were not like the rest of the people. They called themselves *desperados*. There was nothing on the face of the earth they would leave alone. He knew, because he had been a *desperado*, too. They knew him as 'The Tiger'. But now the tiger in him was tamed. It was two years he had been up for. It seemed an eternity. He wondered if they were tamed, too.

He remembered what Little John had shouted to him after the sentence. They had been leading him away then, Little John had shouted : 'We'll get you – if we have to wait ten years we'll get you !'

And heated, he had swung round and had shaken his handcuffs and had said 'Watch you'self Little John ! Watch you'self !' And the people had laughed because he had shaken his handcuffs, and the police had pushed him forward savagely. Then he had been driven away to the train station.

That was two years ago but it seemed like twenty. It seemed long because in jail it took so much to see a day out. It took hunger and the shouts of the warders and it took brutality and a lot of pain.

He wondered if Little John had any ideas about that. Little John liked to talk loudly from the corners of his mouth and he liked to know he was feared, but he had never been to jail. But two years was enough time to cool any man down. He hoped Little John had forgotten things by now. For after a man had been through two years of what he, Willis, had been through, he only wanted to come back to his own little town and live in peace.

Willis walked slowly, his parcel under his arm, looking at the openness and the wideness of the town. He looked, too, at the many people whom he knew and who just passed him by. He was glad they passed him like that and yet he wondered if they had really forgotten. He hoped they had and yet he didn't know that he should. They looked so warm and friendly. He was glad he came back. He walked up the High Street and stopped at an orange-vendor's stall to refresh himself.

In the town the gang had talked among themselves. For the past few days they had been talking. They knew that the Tiger was going to be uncaged – and they were afraid. All except Little John. When he had said he would get the Tiger he had not only been playing brave. He had meant it. For Little John was a real *desperado* and bravado and not like the rest. Many of the gang carried knives and ice-picks and talked from the sides of their mouths but they'd run if a leaf trembled in the dark. Little John feared nothing. Not even the Tiger. There had been times when the Tiger had run wild and had sliced up many of the gang and had got away with it. Some of them carried his trade-mark on their bellies and on their cheeks and behind their ears. But not Little John. He and the Tiger had never clashed but he knew who would carry the mark if they did. He knew one of them would have to carry the mark now. He had waited two years for this. The Tiger must not hold the town at bay any more. Two years ago the Tiger had ambushed Cyril and had used his knife in such a manner that now

Cyril was crippled for good. And he had got only two years for that. If the Tiger was allowed to prowl the town again it would be another time of terror. The rest of the gang would just disappear, because they were already afraid. But he, Little John, was not afraid. He had stayed there and had fumed and boiled up for two years, waiting for the Tiger to be let loose.

And now that the train had come in he had felt all his strength and the lion was awake in him. He had stood in the crowd and had seen the man with the brown paper parcel under his arm step down onto the platform. His heart had pounded. And impatiently he had followed him along the wharf, and then along the High Street. There was a certain arrogance in the way the Tiger had ambled on. It was as if the town was his and he had come back to rule again. Little John had walked behind him impatiently, knowing that sooner or later he must accost him. He mustn't give the Tiger a chance to settle himself. He had to move fast.

And now as the Tiger stood at the orange-stall, peeling and sucking oranges, Little John came up stealthily. He looked at the man sucking the oranges and he was riled almost out of control. Prison had seemed to give this man the easy, cool confidence of veteran criminals. He was standing casually sucking oranges in the town where many carried the marks of his knife and where he had butchered one so mercilessly that his life would never be the same again. Bitterness swelled in Little John. Now was the time to act. He put his hand into his pocket and the sharp point of his weapon answered him. He walked out into the open. 'Tiger!' he cried, 'Tiger!' And the way he shouted it was as if ten lions were roused in him.

Willis turned around. His heart seemed to drop down into his stomach. People passing in the street stopped to look. They looked at Willis and whispered to each other

64

that this was the man. Little John stood there, defiant, raging. No, they didn't forget in this town. No one did. There were more people in the street now. The orange-vendor grew nervous. There seemed to be trouble brewing. Willis looked at the crowd and looked at Little John, advancing. The crowd glared hostilely at him and he knew he couldn't run. There was no avoiding the trouble. The two years he had just had flashed to his mind and for once he was really afraid.

'All right, Little John,' he said. 'What wrong boy, what wrong wid you.'

'What wrong wid me?' Little John screamed back. 'You think I is Cyril? You can't threaten me, Tiger! You can't threaten me and get away! Is either you mince me up or I mince you up!'

The orange-vendor cried: 'Call the police, somebody! Somebody go and call the police!'

Little John was already across the road. There was no way out for Willis. The Tiger who had so long kept the town at bay was himself at bay now. He saw the flash of an ice-pick as Little John lunged at him. Swiftly Willis ducked away, shielding his face. As his face turned he saw the long, sharp blade of the orange-vendor among the oranges. And in that moment of desperation he whipped it from the tray. He was ferocious now. He was the terrible Tiger again. He caught hold of Little John's arm on the swing and brought him crashing on to the pavement. Then he drove the orange-knife in the soft place between the ribs. Blood spouted out. The crowd was in pandemonium and the policemen had to bully their way through, throwing people aside. Two or three of them held the Tiger, locking his arms behind his back. Then they pushed him along to the Black Maria and drove off.

Many Things

❧❧❧

'Chin Tick,' the boy shouted and ran. Then he stood up and picked up a handful of pebbles to throw at the shop, changed his mind, screamed 'Chin Tick!' again, and ran up the hill.

Chin Tick, the new Chinese dealer, had heard the noise. He had been up early, the day being Christmas Eve, and standing on the counter now, he had remained still, the end of a streamer in his hand. He had waited for the shower of stones to fall on the shop. Hearing none, he smiled and went on again with his decorating.

The shouting out of his name had jerked him from his reveries. That boy, he thought. He was in a gay frame of mind. Although he was sometimes angered by the boy calling out, 'Chin Tick,' and then the irritating noise of stones on the shop, this morning the boy's pranks rather amused him. Alwan, he thought. Already he was knowing people's names. He realized Allwyn was getting used to him.

Having tacked on that end of the streamer which he was holding, he jumped down from the counter. He got another roll and climbed onto the chair near the door. There was a lot of red and yellow and now he thought green would look nice. He had been thinking – before the boy had shouted – about this thing called Christmas, and about how the people were so excited about it. He was glad about this because he was only new here and it had helped him to make many friends. From the time the women came into the shop, now, it was – Chin Tick you having ham for Christmas? Chin Tick you having bacon? You having this? You having that?

At first he was puzzled but afterwards he had come to understand it all. Christmas was the great feast, the great event. Like the Name Days in Nanking. Thinking of the Name Days brought a faint longing inside him. On such days they rose early, and there were many gifts exchanged, and much visiting, and many nice things said, and plenty to eat. Seeing how excited the people were here, he knew what Christmas meant to them. It had come to mean something for him, too. He had looked forward, unsure at first, but now it was a big Name Day for him.

There was much yellow and red and green now and standing on the floor he admired the changed appearance of the shop. It brightened him to have the shop aflame with colours, and it brightened him, too, to see the rows of hams and bacon and pickled chicken hanging from strings above the counter. He had stocked his shop well, they all told him so, and this morning when they came in they would see he had brought the hams. He grinned to himself. In Nanking there were no hams but there were hams here and it was good. 'Good,' he said aloud, feeling the English word strange on his tongue. Then he said the Chinese word for good. 'Good,' he said again in English, and grinned again.

It was still too early to open the shop. It wouldn't be time to open for another fifteen minutes. He was thinking about Nanking again but somehow the sharp, quick memory of the boy crossed his mind. 'Mischief,' he thought, thinking the English word. Very few things gave him as much pleasure as the practising of English. It was so early, his shop wasn't open yet, and still the mischievous boy had passed and screamed his name. 'Good-for-nothing,' he thought. He thought of it in Chinese, and it was a very amusing, cutting word, and he wondered how it sounded in English. That good-for-nothing boy, he thought.

He went behind the counter and checked on the barrel of salt meat. Then he brought a full bag of sugar and checked on the bags of rice. It was funny, he was thinking, rice in China and rice here. Mai Ling had made such lovely rice noodles in Nanking. He always thought of Mai Ling, so loving and delicate and sweet now, as she had been on their wedding day. She was, as her name suggested, an opening flower and his heart was always sensitive lest anyone hurt her. She was still lying asleep, enfolded, and he had kissed her on the petals of her eyes and her delicateness had excited his heart. Now that he had done everything and the shop was ready to be opened, he would go in to awaken her. He would go into the room softly, but her eyes would be already opened and she would smile at him. And this morning, as on the mornings of the Name Days so far away, he would greet her according to the Nanking fashion. And she would be surprised, because she would not be expecting it, and she would laugh and be delighted. Emotion was in him as he walked towards the room, trying to remember the two English words that she had liked – the words Mrs Anderson had said to them. Mrs Anderson was a very gentle lady who lived not too far away. This lady had come in a car and had bought things, and had greeted them nicely. He walked now into the little room where the honoured Mai Ling was awakening and he felt the excitement rushing like a river inside him.

The boy, Allwyn, had run up the hill and run back down

they stood before the shop bowing low, replying, Mai's voice ringing out, 'Many Chings!'

But already the boy was a good distance off, running desperately past the red hibiscus of the hedge.

Peeta of the Deep Sea

※※※

Peeta panicked. There was nothing he could do. He was trapped. Trapped with hundreds of others. The Monster had come and was slowly, surely, dragging them from the deep. Peeta swam through the excited crowd to try the bottom. Then he tried the top again. The great Monster had encircled them completely. There were millions of holes in its great hands, but none large enough. If only these holes were a little larger. Peeta tried to push himself through one of the holes again. He squeezed and squeezed. Great tails lashed around him. Not only he but the whole crowd were in desperation. He tried to ease himself through. The threads pressed against his eyes. If only his head could get through. He pushed again, hard, and the pain quivered through his body. Down to his tail. He turned around. But it was no use trying it from that end. His tail was much wider than his head. There was nothing he could do. He heard the breakers roaring above now. That meant they were nearing the shore. Peeta whipped his tail in fury. The Monster was closing its hands gradually. He could feel the crowd heaped against each other. He was knocked about by the giant tails. Good thing he was so small and could avoid being crushed. Around him were his friends and his dreaded enemies. The bonito was there, the killer shark was there. None of them thought of him now. They were all trying to escape.

The killer shark, he thought again. The Monster was

taking the killer shark, too. Shark, bonito, herring, cavali – they were all the same to him. A giant swordfish charged the threads desperately. The shark turned on its belly in vain to swallow the Monster. Instead it swallowed a jelly-fish. There were cries now above the surface. Below, the Monster grated on the sand. The shore! They had reached shore! Frantically Peeta flung himself against one of the tiny holes. He gave a cry as the scales tore from his back – then a cry of joy. He was free! Free!

He lunged forward below the surface. He could feel the weight of the breakers pushing down on him. He could hear the terrible roar which from the deep had sounded like a whisper of music. He looked back a little. There was only a tiny streak of blood behind him. He would be all right. He would be all right. Down, he went. Further away and down. Faster, faster he swam. His tail whipped the white foam, pushing him forward like a spear. Down, he sped, rejoicing in his tinyness. If he was only a little bigger he would have been dying on the shore now. The fateful shore. There had been those who had actually come back from that world. This was one of the greatest mysteries. It was hard to believe that any fish had come back from the shore. But some said they had been there, and had talked of that awesome place of no water, no fish. It was hard to believe this. But so had it been to believe about the Monster. But the Monster was real enough now. His mother had always warned him. He looked back a little. There was no more blood now. Down, down he swam. Deeper, further. Deep, deep, until the sound of the breakers was only a bitter memory, and the sea was not sandy but blue and clear, and until far, far away in the distance, green with the fern and the tender moss, he saw the rocks of home.

A thrill ran through him. He squirted through the water as if a new verve had possessed his body. His tail whipped the white and frothy foam. 'Mother!' he thought, 'Mother!' And he dived headlong towards the green rock.

'Mother, I am home,' he gurgled.

The mother stared at him between the rocks. She noticed the bruised back. She was cross, yet the fact that he had returned made her feel thankful inside.

'Peeta!' she exclaimed.

'I am home,' he said.

'Wherever have you been to? Whatever happened!'

She was sure he had gone playing among the rocks and had lost his way. And that he had bruised his back swimming carelessly or romping with the shingles. Peeta was like that. He always went far away to play. He always ran away to meet the corals and the anemones and his other friends of the deep sea.

'Where have you been?' she said.

'Mother – ' Peeta hesitated, 'Mother – the Monster.'

The mother went cold with shock. Her eyes gleamed white and there was fear and horror in them.

'Peeta, I warned you, I warned you. You wouldn't hear. Why did you go near the surface?'

'Mother – '

'Keep away from the surface, I always tell you. Keep away from the shore!'

'Mother, the Monster is everywhere.'

'He can't come between the rocks. He never comes here.'

'Mother, I can't stay all day between the rocks. I have friends everywhere. This morning I promised the corals – '

'This morning you promised nothing!' gulped the mother. 'You nearly promised your life. Keep here between the rocks. Play with the moss and the fern. Here you are safe.'

'The Monster isn't always here,' said Peeta. 'Sometimes I swim out to my friends. We see the wonderful things. Sometimes we go up to the surface to see the sun. It is dark here below. Up there it is bright and very strange. When I grow up I will go often to see the sun, and to hear the music of the waves, and to watch the winds play on the roof of the sea.'

'Hush up,' the mother gulped. 'It is more beautiful here between the rocks. It is more beautiful here because it is safe. Tell me, how did you escape? It is very odd. No one escapes the Monster.'

'Oh,' said Peeta, and he told her. He told her how he was just playing and how very suddenly he found himself against the great hands of the Monster. He told her how terrified he had been and how he swam down to the bottom to escape, but he could not. And even at the top he could not. For the hands were everywhere. The hands with the million tiny holes. He told her how there were hundreds of others caught like him, even the killer shark. She gulped, and shrank back, and he said yes, the killer shark. And he told her how the great hands had closed gradually around them and pushed them all together, and how they were all frightened and desperate, even the killer shark. He told her how the breakers had pounded over them and how they were dragged on the sands of the shore and how he had actually heard the voices of the shore. Then he told her how he had flung himself desperately against one of the holes, while the threads cut him and the pain shot through him, but how he had discovered himself free at last in the wide ocean. And he laughed as he said this part, for he remembered himself speeding through the water, faster than barracuda, faster than anything.

75

But the mother did not laugh. In fact, she was gloomier than before. For Peeta was a wayward fish. She knew she could not change him. She knew that with all her advice she couldn't prevail upon him to keep away from the open deep, and from the surface, and from the sound of the breakers near the shore. She knew, too, as well as he, that it was his tinyness that had saved him. But he was growing fast. In the next few months he would be no baby any more. She shuddered to think what would happen then if he made such a mistake again. Certainly that would be the end. Yet, as he grew he would become quicker. The carite was perhaps the fastest fish in the sea. But as far as she had heard, the hands of the Monster were deep and wide and stretched far beyond the bounds of speed. Therefore she turned away sadly and swam to a dark corner of the rock to meditate.

The fully-grown carite was, indeed, the fastest fish in the sea. Peeta no longer feared the barracuda, the shark, the swordfish. In the earlier months these had seemed to him so very swift. Now, with his long, streamlined body, he could oustrip them with the greatest ease.

.The mother was so proud. Peeta was as handsome as he was enormous. But he was not so enormous as to be ungainly. Sometimes at play or just to be showing-off he would go past the rocks like a silver flash. And she would smile. Yes, he had grown up but he was still fond of play. And now he was so popular that his friends would not leave him alone. Every day he sported with the dolphins and corals and the anemones. And at night he came back to dream among the ferns.

Secretly his mother would be amused with his tales. Sometimes she stayed up just to hear them.

'Quiet,' she would say, 'Be quiet and go to sleep!' And he would gurgle teasingly among the rocks, and she would listen to his tales of the deep, about his pranks with the pretty corals and anemones. But about his new friend the moonfish, Peeta said nothing. He had met her at the distant rocks.

As the days passed he thought of the moonfish more and more. It was she of whom he dreamed when he lay among the ferns. There he saw her eyes again, sparkling like the crystal depths. There again he saw her tinted scales, gleaming like mirrors of silver. She was Iona, the Pride of the Sea. Thinking of her, Peeta became more and more wistful, until even his mother noticed and was puzzled. But Peeta kept silent. All his friends of the deep knew, though, and together they talked about it. They talked of how Peeta stared blindly into water, and how once he nearly swam in the way of the killer shark. They talked of Iona the Beautiful, and they envied her. For they knew what would be. And now the dolphins waited on the reefs in vain, and the corals, broken-hearted, murmured their low, sad song.

Eventually Peeta spoke to his mother, for he would go away. She wept because she, too, knew what would be. She asked who was this Iona and Peeta was surprised. All the sea knew, he said. In the heights and in the depths. From the waters near the shore, to the waters of the limitless bounds. Even the wonderful moon in the wind-water above the sea knew of her, for they had played together and he had given his magic to her.

He said he would go away to the distant rocks and before many tides he would return. Then would he bring back, he said, the greatest treasure of his days. He would bring to her his bride and her daughter – the Pride of the Sea.

The mother wept a little. For she realized that in this way Peeta was lost to her. And she knew that she could not forbid this marriage even if she had wanted to. Therefore, she warned him again of the open sea, for it was another of the terrible seasons of the Great Hands. And she told him of the ways to go. The ways which were difficult but safest. Then her heart lifted a little, for the marriage was good. As for the Monster of the Great Hands, the Providence which guided Peeta so long would guide him still. She swam through the rocks looking around her. For now she had to prepare a home for her son and for the beautiful Iona, the Pride of the Sea.

The bay was deep and wide and the winds played on the floor of the ocean. It was a beautiful month for fishing, although it was the mating season. In the mating season you did not catch fish plentifully, but if you were young and you went out with the sea calm and the breeze fresh, and with the sun lighting up the palm-fringed shore, sometimes you laughed aloud for the sheer joy of living and you didn't think of the fish at all.

Thus it had been with these fishermen riding the breakers. But now they cast out their nets with some enthusiasm because of the unexpected sight below. Halfway down, the water was foamy and rippling. The sign of fish.

Quickly they encircled the fish. They watched the leaden weights of the nets sink to the bottom. This would make their day. It came almost too easily. They watched each other, for it was unusual to come upon such a school of fish in the mating season.

Soon they were on shore hauling the catch in. They hauled as the fish struggled in the nets and the breakers chattered along the bay. They pulled and pulled still amazed at their fortune, and when the nets dragged on sand and they could see the host of fins and tails flapping and lashing up the water, they were even more amazed and excited.

They dragged the catch right out on dry beach. There were hundreds of fish, and crabs and corals. Even anemones.

'Look,' said one of the fishermen, pulling out a shiny flat fish from the living heap. Nearby a carite beat violently, gulping and leaping about the sand. The fishermen were looking at the shiny fish.

'It's ages,' said the one with the fish, 'years since we brought in one of these.' He held the fish high. Its eyes gleamed as sparkling as the crystal depths and its scales were like mirrors of silver.

'Moonfish,' he said quietly. He was experienced and he knew it. 'Look at her! Pretty, eh?' he smiled. 'Boy, she is the Pride of the Sea!'

The carite nearby beat furiously.

Uncle of the Waterfront

'Uncle!' I cried.

People were still streaming out of the train. The platform was crowded with luggage and travellers. Mother held me back so I wouldn't get lost, and Father, a little bewildered, said, 'Where's Uncle? Where did you see Uncle?'

The next moment Uncle reached us through the crowd. Mother was taken aback with joy. Father smiled sheepishly and his two palms were like one in Uncle's big hands. Then Uncle leaned over and kissed Mother on the cheeks, and after that he swept me up from the ground.

'Hello Celery!' he said, 'Getting big man now, eh? eh?'

We laughed together. He never called me Learie, but Celery. That was an old joke between us.

He put me down again and took the big suitcase from Father and the small one from Mother, and he walked off beaming, leading the way. We soon came out of the train station and on to the main street, and at the moment the whole town was alive before us.

I was excited. I watched the buses and trams and motor-cars flash by along the busy streets, and I watched the houses which were vast and beautifully painted. And beyond the streets and the houses there was the harbour, making a great semicircle before the town. I looked quickly for the ships that were here last Easter, and for those I had seen at other times, but they all looked strange

to me in some way and I could not tell if they were the
ones I knew. I watched the lighters, too, and I thought of
the big, jovial lightermen that were always in Uncle's
house. I wondered if when they saw me they'd be the
same as last Easter and have fun with me again.

I walked on, thinking of all this and not really listening
to the chatter of Uncle and Father and Mother. Sometimes I saw Uncle pause and look back for me and wink,
and then I winked back and laughed. That, too, was
another joke between us.

We could have taken any bus down the main street
but Father and Mother wanted to walk. So we walked
on, for it was very nice being in the town again. Uncle's
place was not far away and as we approached the harbour, almost every person we passed knew Uncle and
stopped to talk with him. And I remember then what the
lightermen had always complained of – that Uncle was
the most popular man in all the town.

A little more walking brought us to the waterfront.
Everything looked big and new and strange as it did
every time we came here, and when we drew near to
Uncle's house, I thought, as I had done a thousand times
before, that it was the finest house I had ever seen. For
indeed it was very large and had two great wings, and
a balcony half way up, and it was painted a light pink
which seemed to match the sunlight of the bay. It was
far grander than the other houses, and those were very
beautiful houses, too. I watched the ironwork around the
house, and was still amazed by it. I saw the high glinting
windows and the balcony rails, and I remembered that
when you stood on the balcony you were high above the
Customs Office and the Harbour-Master's House. I used
to look down upon the Harbour-Master's yard and sometimes I saw the high official whom Uncle did not
like.

Looking across the bay I saw the lighters which were now close by, and the ships with the giant funnels that dwarfed everything. There must have been hundreds and hundreds of ships in the harbour and twice as many lighters. I walked on, looking back, listening to the laughter of the seamen that came clearly on the wind. I looked at Mother and Father, and Father had the same bewildered grin on his face.

When we reached the house, Uncle pushed the gates open and the polished bronze of the gate took Mother by surprise. Uncle stayed back a little to wait for me. I could see the playfulness in him from the way he looked at me.

'See,' he said, pointing to the ships, 'More this time.'

'Yes,' I said, 'From where?'

'All over the place, China, Italy. . . .'

'And from the Casbah?' I remembered he had spoken of Casbahs. 'From Rio, too?'

Then I spotted the dark corner of the house where we had played 'Devils' last Easter. The old sardine can was still there. I used to cry, 'Devil!' Then Uncle would chase me up the steps with the sardine can and desperately I would try to hide myself in the duskiness of the big rooms. 'From Rio!' I screamed now, and then I cried, 'Devil!' and Uncle made a lunge for me as I ran shrieking up the stairs.

No holiday was more exciting. There were so many rooms in Uncle's house that it was easy to get lost among them. Not only *I* got lost, but Mother and Father, too. For our house at Rambert had only two rooms, and I could not count the number Uncle's had. The furniture in the rooms was rich and elegant and Mother looked at each piece and touched some of them and looked at Father unbelievingly. There was a new grand piano in the corner and Uncle dusted it. Then he sat down to it but he talked all the time and never played a note. And with joy, my eyes wandered from Uncle to the many beautiful things around. And it suddenly struck me as very strange that Uncle should flourish like this though he was at home all day. At Rambert, Father worked from early morning to late evening picking the grapefruits of the estate and coming home very tired, but he never brought new things to our house. And every year when the picking slackened he had to send a letter to Uncle and Uncle always wrote back telling us to come.

Perhaps we were lucky that Uncle lived like this because we could come here and stay with him. Uncle was always good. While we stayed here we ate and drank more than we did at Rambert, and all this because of Uncle's kindness. Mother was unusually happy. Sometimes she walked me down to the wharf among the crowds of sailors and merchants and vendors with peanuts and cakes and fruit, and often she bought cakes and we stood on the wharf in the sunlight eating them and watching the ships come and go. We saw how the lighters skimmed away with the breeze, and how the big boats eased up alongside. We noticed also the painted funnels which told where the ships came from. And when we got back home Uncle would be there talking to lightermen or playing cards with them. If he wasn't doing that he would come running after me and we would play at devils in the darkest corners of the house. Many strange, rich things I saw as I ran where the rooms were darkest, and then Uncle would say I was tired and would take me away from those rooms onto the balcony where he would tell me many jokes. He knew the jokes of the Islanders and the jokes of the far-away peoples and he would remember these and tell them all over again. And he would have me choking with laughter until I was too weak to hear more.

So it was sad when our stay ended. We didn't remain as long as we did at other times. For Father came in from the lighters one noonday and whispered a secret to Mother. Mother suddenly put her hands to her heart and then to her head. Then she turned to me and said we were leaving tonight. They both looked shocked, as if their breaths had been taken away. I wanted to ask why we were leaving but Mother said, 'Shut up!' before I even opened my mouth. So I just slunk away and went to look for Uncle. When I came to the room where the lightermen played cards I knocked. 'Unc',' I said softly. Someone opened the door. Uncle was there talking with a strange man.

He was not a lighterman but was dressed in the manner I had seen in the town when the traffic was heavy. I had seen people dressed like that standing in the middle of the street. Uncle's face looked more distressed than Mother's or Father's. He seemed frightened, sitting the way he did in the chair, and he was sweating.

'O, it's the little boy,' he said.

The strange man looked at me. His black helmet fitted deep down on his head in the same way I had seen it in the town. He tried to smile but it seemed very hard for him to do so. He bent down to me, 'Run away,' he said.

I looked at Uncle and I began feeling desperate inside. The man went on writing and looking about the room. He went up to the piano and inspected it carefully and wrote something down in the book. The book was a little black one and his pencil was very tiny. I wondered if they were toys and if he was making fun. But he was not making fun because his face was very grim. I didn't like him because he did not smile even once, and only friendly people came to Uncle's house.

'Uncle,' I said, and whispered that Mother had said we were leaving tonight.

I waited to hear him say it was not true, that he wasn't going to tolerate any such thing. But he did not speak. He sat there and his face looked very strange and I wondered if this was because of the man.

'Learie,' he said at last, 'Go to Mummy a little – go to Mummy and Daddy.'

And then I was sure something was wrong. For Uncle never called me Learie, but Celery. And he never sent me away. I walked silently down the corridor with the low verandah, and the harbour was just in the distance below. The sun was red and it hit slantingly across the ships, and across the lighters, which were rocking a little because they were being unloaded. I wondered who was that man with Uncle.

I did not know but I felt he was the one who was making us leave for Rambert tonight. I went in through the door where Mother and Father were talking. Mother suddenly put her hands to her mouth. But I had heard the word she had said and it dawned on me it was a very funny word. I started to ask Father what it meant but he swung round at me and I said no more. They were hurrying to pack the suitcases. The noise of the harbour seeped into the room. I felt a burning inside. It was a pleasant, beautiful town here, and Uncle's house was the finest I had ever known. Now we were going back to Rambert just like that. I wondered if the word Mother had said had anything to do with the man talking to Uncle and with our going back tonight. But it could not be, for it was such a pleasant, ringing word. I said it quietly to myself. It sounded so strange on the tongue. I itched to say it aloud. I crept away to a far corner and

85

told myself we were going home tonight. And then, softly at first, I said the word Mother had spoken. And then, being careless, I wanted to shout it to the emptiness of the house. So taking a deep breath, I cried: 'SMUGGLING!'

The Sapodilla Tree

❖❖❖

The tree was so laden with sapodillas that the branches bowed down under the weight. The fruits were large and brown and tempting. And with little imagination you could see the rich syrup just settling there under the skin. Some of the fruit was bat-bitten, and the juice there had turned to sugar, with the black currant-like seeds sticking out. And it hurt the heart to watch the over-ripe sapodillas that had fallen under the tree.

But nothing could be done about that, for the real trouble with the sapodilla tree was that it grew just outside Mr Farfan's window. And Mr Farfan was no humble giver. In fact, he was the biggest 'no' man we ever knew.

However pleadingly you asked for a sapodilla it was always no, no, no, with Mr Farfan. And then he would wonder why the young generation was growing up so lawless and greedy and how in his day a child would never be asking for sapodillas. And when he was in a bad spirit, and we were a little stubborn, he would pull out the big stick from behind the door and have us running, screaming, down the road.

Winky and I decided not to ask Mr Farfan for any sapodillas any more. I said I would let him stay there and rot with his old sapodillas! Winky said so, too. But I was surprised when one day Winky came home panting, his hat full of ripe sapodillas.

'Where you get them?' I asked.

'Don't know?' he grinned.

I was astonished. 'He give you?' And then I realized how silly I had been. Mr Farfan would quicker give his soul away than his sapodillas. There was only one explanation to it. Winky had got up early that morning and raided the sapodilla tree.

It was a long time before I could persuade Winky to take me on one of his early-morning visits. I had to bribe him with all kinds of things, and make all sorts of promises to him. Eventually he gave in for my brand new top.

Still, he was very nervous about taking me along. I was not exactly the sort of partner he liked to have when it came to these things. It didn't seem that I was cut out for Winky's role. I was a little timid and seldom efficient. Not so Winky. He would have raided anything at the shortest notice. And he would be so composed you wouldn't think anyone objected.

'Orright,' he said, sizing up the top I offered him, and seeming to weigh things on his mind. 'Orright, we'll go. But for Christ sake take things easy. If you make Farfan ketch us is sure jail.'

The morning was just right when we went. Not too dark, not too bright. Everything was as still as a cemetery.

Winky was to climb and pick the sapodillas and I was to remain under the tree catching, and putting them in the bag. That was all. I felt a little disappointed that there was nothing heroic about it.

Winky sent down the first one, and it slipped through my fingers and burst on the ground. I could hear him fuming in the branches above.

'What is one sapotee!' I cried, hurt.

'You'll know,' he said softly, but acidly, 'Make them fall and wake up Farfan and you'll know!'

We got over that bad patch and things began going

88

smoothly. I was catching better and better. I was even catching some like an expert – with one hand. Whenever Winky saw me doing that he turned a very sour eye upon me.

But we were getting through fine and soon our bag was almost full of sapodillas. I told Winky so. He said, 'Okay, let me send down these last few, quick. Ketch them good, eh?'

And then all at once he seemed to stiffen and grow pale up in the tree. I was taken aback. I called up at him, 'What happen?' He looked at me and then looking towards the house – with fear all over his face – his mouth formed the word *'Farfan'*. Pell-mell I raced down the road.

The day had cleared when I decided to take a walk back. I was worried. I had been sitting at home all the time waiting for Winky. I was waiting to hear the whole epic. Of course, I knew he wouldn't be caught, but I wanted to hear just how he got away. Almost every day Winky added a new chapter of heroism to his life. But it was not so much what he did but the way he told it to you. I always felt that Winky would grow up to write thrillers some day. He had such a way of telling things. Although you might have been there when it happened, it was always a new joy to hear Winky relate the event. And I knew this would turn out to be a real masterpiece. That was why I waited so anxiously for him to come.

But he was a long time coming. The minutes turned to hours, and the day dawned full, and still he didn't arrive. And then it came to me. It came to my head as clear as crystal. As soon as I had fled and Mr Farfan had come outside, Winky had jumped down from the tree, took up the bag, and dashed up – not down – the road. The cheat! He had gone to the black-sage patch, where he usually hid things, swallowing down as many sapodillas as he could swallow, and hiding the rest!

So I got up, not worried any more but angry. Angry and fuming. After all, what had happened wasn't my fault. *I* hadn't made Mr Farfan open the door and come outside!

I walked up the road, anger burning inside me. I was going straight to demand my share. I wasn't going to let Winky take my share of the sapodillas just because he was bigger than me!

Mr Farfan's door was open when I passed before the house. Timidly I glanced in. Then I held my head straight and walked past. 'Morning Ken,' I heard after a few more steps. I started. As I looked, there under the sapodilla tree was Mr Farfan, his stick in his hand and the bag of sapodillas before him.

He was looking across at me and smiling. 'You'd like a few sapodillas?' He dipped his hands in the bag. I was dumb-founded. My eyes travelled from him to the sapodilla tree, then up the sapodilla tree. 'You want a few sapotee?' he asked again, getting up.

But I had already taken off. I ran with everything I had in me, and as I ran the tears streamed down my face. I didn't know why I was crying. Perhaps it was because of the way Winky looked at me from up in the branches that my heart melted now. And I remembered Mr Farfan's big stick. The thought of it made me weak. And I had to stop running and walk the rest of the way home. But I couldn't get Winky out of my mind. I knew it was going to take more than Superman's courage – coming down from that sapodilla tree with Mr Farfan standing underneath.

I was sitting at home, still crying, when I heard a voice outside. I got up in time to see Winky bounding into the yard. 'Get away!' I cried in welcome, wondering how he brought it off.

'None for you!' he said grinning. It was only then I noticed the basketful of sapodillas.

But I didn't say anything. At that moment I wasn't interested in sapodillas. I wanted to know how he brought it off.

'He didn't ketch you?' I asked.

'Ketch me for what?' And then he burst out laughing. He said : 'The man call you and you run.'

I looked at him, puzzled.

He laughed and laughed and then, unable to keep it any longer, he told me the whole truth. I was stunned. Until now, not even the slightest suspicion had dawned on my mind that Winky had been continually making a fool of me – that lately he and Mr Farfan were the best of friends.

The Girl and the River

❖❖❖

There is nobody in all Ortoire who cannot remember the ferry. None save those too young to understand or too old to remember anything at all. For it had been plying the wide river even before the village itself sprang up, in those remote times when men said the river was too wide to take a bridge.

But today there is no ferry any more. No more the precarious platform which took people and vehicles from bank to bank. Nor the winch and cable which drew the ferry across the river. Indeed, if you were travelling that way you'd be amazed by the steel bridge which towers where the ferry used to be. And you'd have been as overjoyed as I was when I was commissioned to build that bridge.

I was overjoyed and excited only until the work began. For at that point the anger of the whole village was unleashed upon me.

Everyone was bitterly opposed to me because of the ferryman. They said I was trying to chase him off the river. They said the ferryman belonged right here in the village and had been working the ferry before I was born. Now I had come – they did not know from where – and I found the ferry not good enough. They would see how far I'd get.

I kept quiet but I was determined to carry on with the work. For I needed a project of this size and the Ortoire river needed a bridge. I could not let the villagers frighten me away. We began by laying the foundations on the banks, driving piles in the riverbed, and cutting back the mangrove. All the time we worked the villagers hurled abuses at us and in the end they threatened to stop us if we did not stop.

We were scared, but fortunately they were never as good as their word and we pushed on with the job. We kept on going relentlessly for we were anxious to finish in the shortest time possible and clear out. We sweated from dawn till dusk and at night we stayed tensely in camp. We had no friends but the river itself, and the crabs of the mangrove, and the birds of passage that came and went.

When after many months the structure began taking shape across the river and the end of our labours drew in sight I began growing so excited I could hardly sleep at nights. And it was not only because I was anxious to be rid of this place. Each time I laid my head down I had visions of opening ceremonies and great crowds, and miles of cars queueing to drive over the bridge. My bridge. This was my first opportunity and I wanted to leave something on the face of the land. I wanted people to see it and know that I had built it and I wanted them to say it was the best in this part of the world. I grew so nervous for the completion that in my spare hours I had to go far from the bridge to find peace inside me. I did not dare show myself in the village so at such times I would take our little boat and row down river, losing myself in the green wilderness beyond the village.

Down river there was a tributary where some of the village folk came to wash clothes. The water was very clear in this part and there was a big, flat stone on the bank. I often came here and sat on the stone – when no one was around – and I would let my mind wander from place to place : to Port of Spain, my home-town; to the problems of this place; and to where and what I'd be sent to next. Very often my thoughts would dwell on this village here, and I would wonder what it was really like, and I would ask myself whether these angry people would change their minds and be pleased when the bridge was finished. I would think about all these things, and after about an hour or so I would get back into the boat and row towards the mother river again, then upstream towards the bridge.

One day, arriving at the stone earlier than usual, I met a young woman scrubbing clothes. I was going to turn back but she looked up and saw me, so I said, 'Afternoon'.

'Afternoon, Mr Danclar.'

I could not remember seeing the face before, but the young lady knew my name. They all knew my name in the village, it seemed.

'Doing some hard work?'

'Yes,' she said.

She was poorly dressed and she seemed anxious for me to leave. But it was the closest I had got to one of these villagers for a long time, and as she seemed the gentle type I wanted to talk. I was interested to know whether she, too, thought the bridge the work of the Devil.

I said, 'The water clean here, eh?'

'That's why we does wash clothes here,' she said.

This drew my attention to the large heap of clothes she had washed already, but there was a still larger heap waiting to be done.

'You could do all this today?'

'Might,' she said, 'but if not, I'll have to come back tomorrow.' She paused a little, her hands frothy with soap. She looked at the remaining bundle, and she looked round at the vast waters stirring about her.

I said, 'Tide coming in.'

'It look so. It must be getting late. I'd better finish, to go.'

She resumed washing and I pretended that I did not notice in her words the invitation for me to leave. I would not leave until I had asked her about the bridge.

She took up another piece of clothes from the bundle. I looked at the heap. She really seemed to be confronting a heavy task and I thought if I could say anything to make it lighter I would. I looked at her. She was busily washing and not looking at me but I could see she was conscious of my being there.

I said, 'You know, I wish I was you. This place is so quaint – so quiet. I like this. I like to work in quietness and peace.'

She said, 'In Ortoire it have too much quietness and peace.'

'Too much quietness and peace? That's what I'm looking for.'

'I don't mean so,' she chuckled. 'I mean the place itself – you know.'

'But tell me, you find here too dull? What's the village like?'

'Well there's nothing much to do in Ortoire. But I like here.'

Now I brought the boat right up to the stone and as I stepped onto the bank, she said anxiously, 'Mr Danclar!'

I was quickly back into the boat and about to push off. She couldn't help laughing at me.

I said, 'It's all right. I don't want you to get in any trouble for me. I have enough myself already.'

She said, 'No, it's not that. It wouldn't look good if anybody see you here. You know what people give. And especially. . . .'

95

'I know, I know. Especially as they want my head in the village. You think I don't know what the position is?'

She couldn't stop laughing. Then she said, 'Don't think I'm against you. I realize you only doing your job.'

'Well, thank you very much. Thanks a lot. Because nobody else seems to realize that.'

She said nothing. I continued, 'After all, I'm only a Government servant come to build a bridge. I don't want to put anybody out of work.'

She kept on washing. 'Don't worry about that,' she said. And after a while she added, 'I see you nearly finish.'

'Praise God,' I said, feeling relief.

She chuckled. 'I know how happy you'll be to leave here.'

'Aha? I'm not so sure about that. Strange, but this place seem to be growing on me. I like this sort of life – trees, river, birds. . . . Somehow I'm growing to like this wilderness,' I said, 'once the Ortoire people leave me alone.'

She smiled. She was rinsing out the clothes now. She said quietly, 'I, too. This place growing on me, too.'

'So you don't belong here, then?' I was surprised.

'Well, yes and no. I from here but I spend almost my whole life in Sangre Grande. But since Pa isn't working now, I'm back here helping him out.'

'But couldn't you work in Sangre Grande and still help him out?'

She hesitated a little and said, 'But I want to be here, too. He's so depressed.' She was looking at the river.

'And where you work now?'

'Right here.'

I just looked at her and could not say anything. Inside,

I felt shocked. At first I thought that this young lady was just the elder sister in a family, taking charge of the week's washing. I did not know that she washed other people's clothes so that she and her father could live!

After a few moments I left the girl and her washing and with a depressed feeling I rowed down into the mother river, and then up to our quarters. I watched the great structure towering across the river before me and for once I did not feel any pride.

Why was life so ironical? I thought. Here across the river rose an engineer's dream of success, and yet on this very river there was also the distress and even humiliation of a young girl.

That night, as I began telling my foreman the story of the girl, I noticed he fell into an unusual silence.

'What's the matter?'

'You know the girl?'

'No, but that doesn't make any difference. I just feel that for a young person the life she's leading is hell.'

'So you having regrets?'

'Regrets about what? I mean I don't get your point.'

My foreman turned and looked at me and said, 'Now don't give me that, Shallo. Don't try to play you don't know what's happening.'

'You mean something special happening? Something besides. . . .'

He was laughing heartily. Afterwards he said, 'Anyway, the point is, we came here to build a bridge and we almost finish it. This place more than need a bridge and even the ferryman himself will realize this in the end. Although everybody vex like hell now. But to come back to this girl – I can't believe you don't know her because she belong to right over there. In a sense she's doing that job because of the bridge. But what the hell. The old man won't last long and she can go back to

97

Sangre Grande and look for a job. Let's face it, the old man couldn't do that job much longer anyway. Just imagine your father – a man of about eighty – pushing a big donkey of a plank across a river !'

The Holiday by the Sea

❖❖❖

'Ah!' said the young doctor contentedly. He got up and looked along the road through the palms. Then he lay down on the sand again and smiled to himself. He was enchanted by the idyllic scene around him and his early morning swim had given him extra verve.

He felt such a new man these days. It was as if he had asked for a new body and it was given him. Strange what a difference two weeks could make – two weeks of peace and freedom and good food. All that he had been concerned about before were books, drugs, and experiments; and the environment he knew was the bustle and clutter of Port of Spain.

There he spent his life listening to an unending stream of complaints – complaints of pains, bruises, heart troubles, nervous breakdowns, run-downs – every possible affliction. He had examined and had prescribed for all. And in turn he, too, had become tired and run-down, so that he felt he could continue no longer. And then he had prescribed for himself. But he had not prescribed quinines, or injections, or 'shake well' medicines. No. On a friend's advice he had prescribed one month at Mayaro, by the sea.

Again he got up and looked along the road beneath the palms. He could not see anyone and he lay down on the beach again. He said to himself, 'Joe ain't coming or what!' He rolled on the sand and then he got up and tried in vain to touch his toes, bending. He groaned, and gave up. Then he raced down towards the water. He dived and swam underneath, then he stood up and turned to look through the palms again. A wave curled up and crashed on him, tumbling him many times over.

Joe arrived at last. He arrived in his bathing pants and with a cutlass, and he and the doctor bathed together a little and then they went on their usual jaunts.

They did not go following seine boats this morning. Instead they went to a part called Lagon Mahoe where there were low coconut trees with big, green, nuts. But after Joe took the trouble to climb, the doctor could only drink one. Joe was so surprised. He said, '*One*. Doc?' The doctor replied, 'Yes, one. I ain't able this morning, boy.' Joe laughed.

As Joe peeled one of the nuts for himself the doctor turned and looked out at the bay. There were many seine boats out there, dipping and rising, and there were the froth-crested waves seeming to break over the boats. He was absorbed in looking at this and Joe followed his gaze and said, 'Fish, Doc? You change you mind?'

'Not really. Let's give it a little rest today.'

The doctor did not like turning this down because he knew how scarce fish was in Port of Spain. But here, everywhere you turned was fish. Fish to go with fish, it was as bad as that, he smiled. He knew he was not being fair because this was also the place of chip-chip, and bread-fruit, and ground provision. He did not even want to think of food. But he wished he was not fed up with fish because with Joe following the seines he did not have to pay a cent. But the truth was the truth.

He turned to Joe, 'What about Mr Abraham?'

'He coming this evening.'

The doctor was relieved. Mr Abraham was Joe's friend and he always went hunting and brought wild-meat.

Now the doctor said to Joe, 'What about crab hunting?'

'In the mangue?'

'In the mangrove, anywhere.' The doctor looked keen.

'Right. But you know you wouldn't get the blue-backs there you know.'

'Is orright,' the doctor said.

Joe picked up the cutlass from the sand. 'Let's go,' he said. Then he dashed off. 'I'll race you to the river,' he cried. The doctor gave chase.

Crab hunting became one of the regular hobbies of the doctor and Joe. The doctor liked it for the fun and for the crabs, and he always got Joe's mother to make callalloo with the crabs, and on these occasions at dinner he licked his lips for callalloo was one of the things he had not had since he was a boy. Now, too, the doctor began going hunting with Mr Abraham and what really fascinated was what he called the 'Wonderland' of the high woods. There he saw so many things that were new and strange to him. He learned what a manicou was like and there was where he got introduced to the agouti that he had always read about. And one day he heard Mr Abraham say, 'By Christ! I have to ketch a tatou today.' And it flashed back to him from across the years that he had once seen a picture of a shelled beast, and below were the words: *Armadillo or tatou*. He said to himself: 'And to think I born in Trinidad.'

Apart from the wild animals, there were various herbs, too, that Mr Abraham showed him. He felt ashamed that being a doctor he had not seen these herbs before. That is, growing. In fact, his greatest embarrassment was to see senna pods on trees and to recognize neither the pods nor the leaves because he did not realize that senna grew in this country.

Yet, what he had come to this village for, he was getting, and in abundance. He felt he had never lived so well, and certainly he never looked so well. His sunken cheeks had filled up as round as ever, and, more than that, he had been gaining weight. But his weight was in muscles, not in fat. Exercise saw to that. He kept going hunting with Mr Abraham but now it was merely for the fun, not for the wild-meat. For he had grown fed up of wild-meat, too, although he did not want to say so. But Joe noticed, and then he had to admit it. He said, 'Joe, you mightn't agree with me, but too much of a good thing, oh, gosh!'

Joe asked, 'But you like here?'

'What? You asking that so easy!' The doctor cried. 'You can't beat this place for a holiday. You can't beat Mayaro by the sea.'

But in the midst of his idyll the month ran out on him and his stay at the seaside came to an end.

Three long months had slipped by since Mayaro by the sea. The office at Henry Street in Port of Spain was going strong again. The young doctor was back and prescribing for all. At the moment, the patients and their complaints filled the waiting room. The doctor was treating patient after patient, and in the meantime dashing in and out, sending for instruments, despatching stretcher cases, and the like.

All signs of his last holiday had worn out. The cheeks were sunken and drawn as they had been before. Veins were showing up on his hands and neck.

His assistant came up and whispered to him. With a puzzled look the doctor peeped into the waiting room.

The assistant said, amused. 'Came a long time now. Said he wanted you.'

The little boy was there sitting on the bench in the

102

waiting room. He was wearing the familiar striped shirt with the big patch in front and with the sleeves threadbare. His tight khaki pants, chafed and discoloured by the trunks of coconut trees, looked even tighter on him now, and shorter – for he had grown a little. He also had his old brown felt hat cocked up on his head.

Joe cut such a ridiculous figure that the young doctor could hardly believe his eyes. And yet this was the same child that had fitted in so well with Mayaro by the sea. At this moment, with the doctor's head filled with medical problems, Mayaro was only a dream, in spite of the boy sitting there. Only the patients and their problems were real.

The doctor said to his assistant. 'Are you sure he said he wanted me? Are you positive?'

The boy in the waiting room heard the word 'positive' and he sprang up from the bench.

'Doc,' he said, 'Where you? I only hearing but I can't see you. Is me, here. Joe!'

The uncouth voice reverberated in the surgery and now the doctor had to step out into the waiting room. The boy ran to embrace him, the soiled hands on the doctor's spotless smock.

Joe said, 'I ain't able with them. I left Mayaro first thing this morning. I bring water-nuts, wild-meat, everything. Even blue-back.' And he laughed aloud, the sound echoing in the silence around him.

The Captain of the Fleet

❈❈❈

At last Don José Maria Chacon got up from his office desk.

He was greatly relieved. It was unheard of to be working on a day like Christmas Eve. Had this been Sevilla, for weeks now he would have already joined in the festivities. Here, in the Trinidad, it was work day and night; signing papers, strengthening the military, and receiving deputations from the common people. His face which had begun to knit into a frown, relaxed now, then spread into a bright smile. Truly enough, it was great to be Governor of the Trinidad.

On his way from the state-room he came on to the balcony and looked at the town. His eyes found the great clock of the plaza. Ten-thirty. Ten-thirty on Christmas Eve morning and Don José just finished work in the state-room! He laughed at himself. You must be getting old, he said. And then he said, next week will be the new year. What will 1796 bring? Will I be recalled to Spain, for instance? He shuddered at the idea. He did not know why, but he was always making such frightening remarks to himself. He thought now of the heaps of papers on his desk. He hoped everything was in order. It was impossible to tell! There is no way of knowing, he told himself. And then he said, 'Holy Virgin, let all be well!'

Don José had known of the British fleet in the Caribbean. There was the French fleet also, just off Martinique. They, the French, were the more dangerous but the

British were the trickier. The only hope was that these two would not combine against him. He had written home for a few more ships and fighting men. Everything had gone well so far. The young king was very pleased with him. He had hoped the papers on his desk were all right. What would 1796 bring?

And then he said sharply, 'Don José!' It was his way of pulling himself together. He was musing and there was hardly the reason to muse. He was a man refreshing and merry by nature. Also, he was blessed with one of the most beautiful women to come out to the islands.

In a few moments he would go into his sitting room. Antonia, the maid, would have already set the drinks out. If he had any sorrows this was the day to drown them. He would drink in the name of the infant Christ, and he would celebrate the fortunes of Spain.

Cheerfulness returned to the face of Don Chacon and brightened it. He stood on the concealed balcony of the great white palace and looked down at the town. The voices of the people below, and the clatter of donkeys' hooves came up to him. The houses with new curtains looked clean and bright, and far beyond them – beyond where the hills had dipped – he could see a ship in the gulf. His heart lifted. Yes, another ship. This was his new capital. They had criticized him, but he was right. The ships could not come in to inland San José. One must think of these things. One must always choose a port for the capital town. In this way news arrived as speedily as possible. What news did this one bring?

He presently became aware of a shadow and spun around.

'Carlotta!'

'It is Christmas,' she said.

'You have not slept late today.' His face was a picture of laughter and surprise.

105

'No, it is Christmas.' Her long, black hair fell upon her shoulders and her dark eyes looked up at him and there was a full, happy smile on her face. He had previously thought of her as the loveliest woman to set foot in the Colonies – now he knew she was the most beautiful woman in the world. He was overjoyed in a strange way. All the thoughts of the depleted armada, and of the French and British fleets, and of this year of intrigue – 1795 – and of the new capital, and even of young Carlos IV, were fled now, blown into nothingness. His wife seemed more ravishing and more tempestuous in her beauty than she had ever done before, and yet she was only smiling quietly at him. This morning she had awakened early and she had taken great pains to prepare herself. Don José put his hands caressingly on her hair, and then as he was about to sweep her to him, Antonia, the maid, came up.

'Someone,' she said. 'An admiral or someone.'

Don Chacon recovered his balance. Then he said, 'Show him in.'

When Governor Chacon set eyes on the stranger, his heart seemed to unhang within him. For a moment he stood there staring in disbelief. He was not sure if it was pleasure he felt, or contempt, or anger, or if it was just the shock of seeing this long-lost man again. He did not take long to find out. He had been surprised beyond words, but after a while he said, 'Señor Alberto, if I'm right.' He was right and he knew it. He had deliberately said 'Señor' although the man wore the uniform of the Captain of the Fleet. He could not concede 'Don' to him. Had it just been someone he had passed by in the streets of Sevilla, and who had now called to pay his respects, he would have fallen on him and embraced him, but this Alberto, this scoundrel, this shameless breaker of women's hearts. . . .

106

The Governor had to stop thinking this way for fear he could not control himself.

Don Alberto's face was filled with wonder and amazement. In one glance his eyes took in the luxurious room, resplendent with brass and velvet and great Castillian pictures. There was a picture of Carlos IV, with that playful glint in his eyes. Don Alberto looked at it and was very impressed. There seemed to be some subtle bond between this man Chacon and the King of Spain. Don Alberto took special pride from this. These observations took only a moment and now his eyes again held the man who had so risen in the world.

'They told me you were in the Trinidad.'

'I am here,' Chacon said, trying to smile.

The boyish grin on Don Alberto's face perplexed Chacon and revived memories that had been asleep. Don Alberto went on, 'It is many years – and now they made you Governor.'

'I have been here ever since I left Sevilla. Did you not know of the appointment?"

They were playing a game with each other. Events which had caused Chacon to seek the appointment had led them to quarrel bitterly.

'I think I remember,' said Don Alberto. 'You caught the coach to Burgos, and you sailed from Cadiz. It seems such a long time. It is good to see you, Don José.'

'It is good to see you, too,' Chacon said, and strangely, he felt something like that. He was growing more and more curious about Alberto. In spite of the boyish mischievous face, and the eyes taking in a thousand things at once, this man seemed no fake captain and he wondered what good times had fallen upon Alberto since that Sevilla coach had rolled away.

But he was anxious to impose his dignity as Governor –

as the man representing the King of Spain – and all he said was, 'How have you fared?'

'Well,' answered Don Alberto.

Don Chacon had been expecting a full reply. People were always anxious to give full replies and crave his favours, but here was this nonchalant low-born seaman being abrupt! He did not lose his poise but he glanced at Alberto's face to ascertain that he had answered with curtness. Don Alberto's face looked warm and friendly and there was not the slightest trace of malice upon it. Governor Chacon felt a little remorseful and said to himself, 'Why are you remembering past things? You have a big heart, why can't you forgive him? You can afford to be indulgent because you have all powers in your hands. And besides, she is now the Governor's wife.' He did not chuckle at this, but, virtuous though he was, he could not help feeling a little disdainful. And then he thought to himself, 'He is the magnet of beautiful women, but Chacon's magnet had more power.' Thinking in this way, Don Chacon lost all his humility and felt badly about it. The truth was that past events of Sevilla were rekindled in his mind.

When Antonia came in with the drinks and went away again, Don Chacon felt better and he persuaded himself to good thoughts.

Now he said, 'Señor Alberto, you are from the ships?'

Don Alberto smiled. He had a dazzling smile and he looked very handsome and he was very brown from the sun. His officer's uniform was stiffly starched and he was wearing the ribbons of the Captain of the Fleet. The Governor felt ridiculous and his face reddened.

Don Alberto leaned forward and poured out two drinks of wine. 'Merry Christmas, Don Chacon. Yes, I am from the ships.'

Then Chacon ventured: 'Privateering?' He let fall

the word as if to suggest there was nothing wrong with privateering and that in any case it was nobody's business.

Alberto was quite easy. 'Everything. I am in the service of the King of Spain.'

At this they couldn't stop themselves from laughing, and Don Alberto raised his eyes to the portrait of the smiling King. This made things even more amusing to him.

Chacon had poured himself another drink, and he felt it warm his throat nicely in going down.

'And so am I,' he said, 'I, too, am in the service of the King of Spain.'

'But as Governor.'

Chacon shrugged his shoulders, but he was very content inside.

'You like it?'

'It is very pleasant.'

'And you are not lonely down here?'

'I have . . .' Chacon fumbled and coughed. Whatever he did Carlotta must not be mentioned here. Alberto added shrewdly, 'You have much to occupy your time.'

'It is as I was about to say. The wine makes one cough.'

'Yes, it is a very nice wine.' And then Alberto said suddenly, 'Your seas are very dangerous.'

Don Alberto was indeed a privateer, one of the grey wolves of the Carib Sea. He had no fleet but the galleon anchored offshore, and now he was hunting just one more prize, then he would ride the trade-winds to Spain. But it was not easy getting away.

Don Chacon understood the remark about dangerous seas. He waited for Alberto to go on.

'They are like the barracudas,' said Alberto. 'No honest ship is safe without convoy.'

'And you are heading for Port Royal?' Don Chacon

suggested. Port Royal was the den of the privateers. Don Chacon was very subtle.

'I am heading for Spain.'

The Governor looked up. He did not expect this. As far as he was concerned the arrangement was most agreeable. Whenever his eyes rested on this bronzed, athletic man, his thoughts, in spite of himself, flowed back to that long-past unpleasant time at Sevilla. He looked upon Alberto now and said, 'When do you sail?'

'Tonight.'

'You shall have convoy,' he said.

If Alberto was deceiving him about going home to Spain, this was the best means to ensure he deceived himself. 'You shall have convoy until daybreak.'

Don Alberto was excited but tried to appear calm. He thanked the Governor, but without profusion, although the sincerity of it touched Chacon, and he was pleased.

'I saw your ship – is that your ship out in the Gulf?'

'Yes, Don Governor.'

'This is my new capital – the port of Spain. I must be careful how ships come into this port,' he said jokingly. His face was red again, but this time with the drinking. He poured yet another drink of wine.

'Merry Christmas to you,' he said.

'Merry Christmas.'

'Merry Christmas.'

'Merry Christmas, Don Chacon.'

Carlotta had ordered the maid into the bedroom and the door was locked behind them. The maid had been looking suspicious all morning and then she had let something slip from her tongue which had alarmed Carlotta.

Carlotta looked aggressively now at the maid. 'What are you talking about?'

110

'He is a good man,' Antonia said.

'Antonia!'

'The Governor is a good man.'

There was some silence.

'What are you talking about?'

There was silence again.

Antonia stood against the wall looking at nothing in particular, then she said, 'It's no use, I know all about it.'

At this stage there was no doubt about that. Carlotta saw it all over her face. And there was only one way she could have known.

'Where is the letter?'

'It is where you left it. I did not take it away.'

'It was addressed to Señora Chacon.'

'I know. You left it on the dressing-table, so I read it,' said the maid bluntly. She had never spoken like this before.

'Yes, I know,' Carlotta said.

They were talking not as mistress and servant but as woman to woman. Antonia had a great advantage and she felt her importance. She said nothing.

'Does he know about it?'

'If he had, would he be talking with the scoundrel?' Carlotta knew she couldn't get angry but had to keep a cool head.

'Governor Chacon is a gentleman,' Antonia repeated defiantly.

'He is a gentleman? How about this – he stole me!'

Carlotta was breaking new ground with her maid. It was all she could do short of pleading with her. At first she had thought of bursting into tears, but she could not sink to that depth when there were other things. After all, it was still Christmas Eve and she was still the Governor's wife.

111

'How about that?' she repeated. 'I belonged to that Don Alberto there, whom you saw. Yes, that very Don Alberto. Your gentleman Governor bribed my parents and then bribed his way to the Governorship. All this to get me away from Alberto. Do you think I am for sale? Do you think José could buy a woman like me?'

'No,' Antonia said. She said it more through astonishment than reason. She could not believe what she was hearing. It was Christmas and she did not know if it was all a performance. It was not a performance for she had been reading letters for weeks. She could not read well but she could still pick up the gist of what was there. Also, owing to the ink stains on the bedsheets she had known why Carlotta always remained late in bed. This was not a performance – this was a *scandal*. She put her hands to her mouth.

Carlotta had drawn closer to her now. 'Antonia, this Don Alberto here wants nothing of me but myself. You know I have much jewellery.'

Antonia turned a shocked face at Doña Chacon. She was a maid but she was no fool. She knew what was implied in those words. She did not say anything but the look she gave said quite plainly that she, at least, could not be bribed.

Yet inside her there was warmth and sympathy. One never saw jewellery such as the Governor's wife possessed!

Antonia said: 'One thing about that Don Alberto, he is a man to look at. . . .'

'You will not be in need,' Carlotta went on.

'. . . I mean, he is not portly, like Don José, although. . . .'

'Stop speaking in this manner,' Carlotta said firmly. She had noted, of course, the influence of the jewellery, so now she felt free to put the maid in her place.

112

But Antonia knew her importance and she was determined. 'I merely said he was handsome, which is a good thing. When are you intending to sail?'

'It is not proper to. . . .'

'When are you sailing, Señora Chacon?'

'Tonight.'

'That will be arranged,' Antonia said.

She stalked out of the room, seriously now, her mind alight with the drama and with the gold.

That night, when darkness fell, the Governor of the island was asleep. His old acquaintance, Don Alberto, had supped with him, and they had agreed to drown old misunderstandings in the rich ruby wines of Spain. When the Governor was drunk Antonia had put him to bed.

Now, outside the palace, the port of Spain was serenading Christmas. There were the long Castillian candles on the window sills and the voices of the flamenco singers came shrilly, pitched high against the strumming of the guitars and against the night.

There were many people in the plaza, and in the road that led to the waterfront.

Don Alberto had already lifted anchor. His ship was a trimmed galleon disguised as ship-of-the-line. In normal circumstances, no ship like this would dare sail into the open Caribbean, but this one, carrying a document with the Governor's hand and seal, was entitled to full convoy until daybreak. Then, the Atlantic Wash should not be far away.

The sails were beginning to take the wind. Don Alberto went down the ladder into the cabin. Then after a moment, two people came up the ladder. They watched the island begin to slide away. They were silent.

Then Carlotta looked at him. Her heart was thumping. 'Don Alberto Ricardo, why are you sad?'

113

'I am not sad,' he said. He was close beside her and she saw his eyes flickering like small lightning.

'What is tomorrow?' he said.

'Tomorrow it is the Christmas.'

'Then kiss me,' she said.

The Village Shop

***

When Moon Peng died and Ma Moon Peng took over the shop, she ran things with an iron hand. For really, Moon Peng had been easy and indulgent, and could not say 'no' to people wanting credit. The result was that in ten years the leading grocery had come almost to a standstill. Indeed, no more did the long strings of onions and hams and bacon hang in front of the shop door. And within the shop itself, apart from an item or two, the monotony of empty shelves was unbroken.

Ma Moon Peng was determined that the shop should thrive again. While her husband was alive she did not quite realize what was going on because things had seemed so calm and secure. It had never occurred to her that life could change – that the peace Moon Peng gave her would not be there forever.

But Moon Peng died. And as if that was not enough, he had left utter confusion behind. Almost bankruptcy. Looking through the papers Ma Moon Peng was appalled to see the state of things. Scores of large accounts by customers were never settled. Many of these people had long since left the village. Some had died. And the few who were still around made her know that their accounts were with *Mr Moon Peng* – not with her.

So she had consoled herself, and had resolved to start afresh. And from then on she had hardened her heart. When Moon Peng was alive, he had had to keep her and look after her, shop or no shop. That was his duty.

But now she had to keep herself. She could not afford to fail.

Ma Moon Peng did not have to remain alone. She was still in the spring of life and many men found a beauty in her. But when Moon Peng died, a certain fire had died within her. She could not love another man as she had loved Moon Peng.

So naturally she had paid no mind to the tender voices and the scented letters that had followed fast on the death. She had no time for love. All her thoughts were given to the affairs of the shop. She would bring it to life again.

So after the month of mourning, when she reopened the business, there was a little sign for all. It stood in bold writing against the newly-stocked goods. It said: CASH TODAY, CREDIT TOMORROW.

This infuriated the village people. They met in the streets and talked about the sign and they shook their fists at the shop. They said this Moon Peng woman played little lamb while Moon Peng was alive but now she was coming out as the beast she really was. The little scamp, they called her. They said if Moon Peng was still alive he'd have dealt with her, putting up a sign like that! And finally they decided that if they could not get credit they would never set foot in that shop again.

The trial of strength started. The quiet, easy-going village folk who had seemed capable of nothing better than thriving on Moon Peng's soft heart, fought stoutly to bring Ma Moon Peng down. They dug the neglected gardens for the tannias, cassava, and eddoes, and they planted with a new spirit. And when the shop goods were absolutely necessary, they went by bus to the nearest town.

Week after week, month after month, they made the sacrifice. It was a bitter one, yet they took courage, for revenge was sweet. Whenever they went past the shop they held their heads straight, glancing in only to give a ferocious scowl at the lonely figure within.

Ma Moon Peng's trade ground to a standstill. The great round cheeses turned rancid, then spoiled altogether. The salt-fish began to rot and the cans on the shelves rusted. Even the barrels of snout and hogs-head showed unpleasant signs of decay and had to be got rid of.

Ma Moon Peng knew she had lost. Behind the card, CASH TODAY, CREDIT TOMORROW, almost every item she had stocked before the reopening of the shop stood in its place. The dust of months lay thickly on the shelves – for although she had always been tidy before, Ma Moon Peng had now forgotten tidiness. Her mind was in confusion. Several times she had looked at the sign to take it down, but always she had hesitated. Taking it down was not all. She would have to make her peace. Although she was a proud woman, she was not above making peace. But after that, what would happen? It would be the same old story. Hundreds of dollars of credit and no payment. That was what the people wanted. If they held out so fiercely for credit it was clear they did not mean to pay. And in the end the result would be no better. Bankruptcy, ruin – Ma Moon Peng alone facing the storm!

Then she made the big decision. She cried, and strengthened herself, for it was not easy. Not for a woman on her own. There was only one thing to do now. Go back to China! She would sell out as soon as possible and go home.

Lee Wah's letter followed quickly on the 'For Sale' notice. When it had first come Ma Moon Peng had dismissed it with one reading. Now she turned up all the letters in the drawer looking for it again, for she remembered it as being the clearest and most straightforward.

Still, it was always so with the Cantonese.

She found the letter and read it again to see how high the offer was. It had better be good, she thought, with some firmness. Cantonese or no Cantonese she wasn't selling below the price!

As it turned out, she was a little disgusted after going through Lee Wah's letter. She wasn't interested in whether his father had once owned that shop or not. He did not own it now. If Lee Wah wanted to buy she was going to sell. But at her price – that was all.

Poon Ting's letter, too, was a disappointment. Although his offer was the highest, there were too many conditions, and big words. And of course she had known about Poon Ting. Although his proverb was 'Chinee for Chinee,' he had squeezed scores of Chinese dealers out of business. He was the biggest schemer ever to leave Hong Kong.

She did not know what to think. One could not trust anybody these days. She put her hands to her head, sighed, and after a pause tapped Lee Wah's letter towards her again.

And that night, dejected, she went into the little room. She lit the candle and drew the writing things towards her. And she put her hands to her head again, in thought. It was long before she threw off her dejection, but when she did she was not weak, and her lips were pressed firmly together. Like an auctioneer's, after the hammer was brought down. She wrote the letter, then she put on her Canton slippers and went out into the street to the post box.

Lee Wah arrived. He was very busy, looking about the shop. That was, of course, when Ma Moon Peng's eyes were turned away. For the delicate loveliness of Canton women was a peril to men like himself – and no flame

118

had died in Lee Wah. But he had honour, and spoke only about the shop, and told of how much he was attached to it.

Lee Wah's offer rose and became so reasonable after inspecting the shop – and inspecting Ma Moon Peng, when she was not watching – that the widow was more than satisfied. Nevertheless, when they were ready to write out the papers, the table was brought out into the hall and the doors and windows were opened wide. For Ma Moon Peng had honour, too, and was careful regarding what people said about her.

Not long afterwards the sign that hung in front of the shop was removed. In its place hung the sign: ASSOON LEE WAH, LICENSED TO SELL WHOLESALE AND RETAIL.

The village was jubilant. Not only had they forced Ma Moon Peng to sell out, but they had got back a Lee Wah – 'Little Lee Wah' – whom they remembered as a child running about old Lee Wah's shop. That was ages ago, but they never forgot the old man. He was an angel of a shopkeeper – until he had got broke and disappeared. God had made few shopkeepers like him. Another of the best – old Peng – had just passed away.

So when they saw the new sign, and later, the fat-cheeked Chinese man in the village, they were overcome with gladness. They went and shook his hands and told him how pleased they were, and some of the women even embraced him.

And he was touched and very happy. They asked him about the old man and if he was still alive, and if he had another shop. And they told him about Ma Moon Peng. He said, 'Forget Ma Moon Peng, Me, Lee Wah, in charge now. Me, Lee Wah!' They laughed and were very pleased. And anxiously they asked when the shop would open, and he said, Monday. They were as excited as children, and could hardly wait.

On Monday morning the shop opened. The people gasped. Here again was the leading grocery! Every shelf was stocked full. Onions, bacon and hams, hung thickly over the doorway.

And, of course, the impudent sign: CASH TODAY, CREDIT TOMORROW, was no longer there.

Lee Wah leaned against the counter in all his glory. He grinned widely to his customers, and he looked often towards the new section – the bar. But it was not the glitter of the wines and rum and whisky he looked at. For the loveliness of Canton women was fabled throughout the world. So looking towards the glitter, he smiled at his new love, Ma Moon Peng.

The Distant One

❖❖❖

It didn't seem such a long time that Albert was away. At least not a year. How the months had flown! A year since Albert was packing, since. . . .

The boy sat up on the bed with the scene vivid in his mind. He relived all the excitement, and pain, and the emptiness of the days that followed: they all came back to his mind this morning. Really, they had never left him. But this morning the pain cut deeper, and the emptiness was more complete.

The other members of the household, though, were up and stirring. The other children had already changed from their night clothes, and were getting busy as usual. The mother hurried about the house, sweeping, dusting, and dashing into and out of the kitchen. Once or twice she glanced from the corner of her eyes at the little boy sitting there on the bed. Now she glanced again and he was still there. 'I wonder what's Leroy's intention this morning!' she said aloud, half to herself, and half sharply; but she went about her chores.

Leroy had indeed been day-dreaming. If any sound came to him it must have come from far away. For his own spinning top was in his mind's eye.

He was recalling the very morning that top was made. He could see Albert now, bending over the lagnette wood, chopping, chopping, until gradually – almost magically – a brand-new top was born. Then Albert had taken a nail from his pocket, moved over the fire-place to heat

121

it, and as easily as ever he had made the hot nail go into
the wood. He had got the exact depth, then he put the
top in water to cool the nail off. Then he had said,
'Here, Lee, try it out!' And Albert had watched Lee put
on the marling twine, and when he had released the top
from the twine with a zing, they were both amazed to
see how perfectly it spun, and for him it was the best
top in the world. 'It's yours, Lee!' Albert had said then.
Leroy had been so surprised and glad that words failed to
come. From that moment it had come home to him that
he and Albert were real, real pals, closer than anything.

All these thoughts were flooding back to him now and
he was completely carried away.

'Leroy!'

The mother's voice was sharp, almost thunderous, so
that the boy, completely startled, felt his heart jump. But
the next moment he had regained his senses and was now
hustling out of his pyjamas and hurrying into home
clothes.

The mother did not have to say any more because
Leroy's task was clear cut.

He was out into the yard now. He hurried to the goats
– for he should have already been on his way to the
tethering place – and though the top was in his pocket,
this morning there would be no time for a *one-line*
game.

The morning sun had already struck the pitch road.
He felt the surface warm and pleasant to his feet. The
goats must have felt the same, for instead of walking on
the roadside grass, they walked in the centre of the road.
Albert had never pulled them away when they walked
in the centre of the road. Only when a car came hurtling
up. And in the evening when he went for them again
he did not have to lead them for they knew the house
and were anxious. And they trusted Albert. When he

122

stood up they stood up, too, and when he started again they started. And now the goats were here and Albert was not here, and the sun made it warm underfoot. That was funny. The boy smiled wistfully to himself, and he could not help wondering whether the sun made it warm under Albert's feet, too, this morning, wherever he was in that England place.

It was different when the last letter had come. Albert had said it was not too bad but it was cold. He had mentioned that there was so much to see and so many places to go to, and it would have been very nice had it not been cold. And then he wrote to ask about Leroy. With this thought the boy felt a sharp pain, which, though he was not tired, made his breath come in gasps. He remembered the letter vividly for he had taken it to school with him and must have read it a hundred times. He and his friends. He had been so proud, but now it was already a long time.

He must write to Albert. He had tried several times but whenever he took up the pen he could not find words to say. But he must write. For Meggy had kids again, and one had died. And the mango trees in Spring Flat were yellow with fruit. And the top – he hung his head, for he would not tell about the nail-hole – the top was still good and he wouldn't play *one-line* with it!

Were it not for the goats he might have walked on past the savannah. But the goats turned off the road, almost dragging him with them. 'Scamps!' he said, as if he realized they had a point on him. And he looked for where the grass was greenest and began driving in his stakes.

The mother tried to be her usual self in spite of everything. She was always up and doing, busy as ever about the house. She made it a point of duty to be so. For she realized that not only did she have to take Albert off the children's mind but off her own mind as well. She could not have carried on if she had allowed the terrible longing to take possession of her. The boy had gone away for a few years only. He had been determined to go and he had worked and had saved his own money. She hoped he made good there because she had counted on his coming back and helping her with the smaller ones. And naturally she was longing to see him again. In the first place, it was not easy letting him go.

She always thought of him but she had fought hard to suppress her feelings. Especially in the light of the children, and particularly so in the light of Leroy, who, if given a moment to himself, would fall into brooding and dream.

She roused herself from her thoughts. Was she not dreaming, too? She busied herself sweeping out the house and then she went outside to wash some clothes. Then she went in and took up the shop-bag as she heard the drone of the mail-bus. She would go to the shop first, then in coming back she would look in at the Post Office. She would not have to go in for she was sure the lady in the Post Office would look out and signal 'No'. Or maybe. . . . Who knows?

As it turned out the lady in the Post Office looked out and signalled 'No'. The mother turned back with pain and took the road up the hill. Seeing that she was broken-spirited the lady in the Post Office called out, 'Perhaps tomorrow, Mrs Austin'.

Mrs Austin turned back and forced a smile. 'Perhaps. I'll send the little boy.'

There were no letters that week. Nor the next week, nor the next. But some time in the following week the Post

Mistress looked out for when the boy was passing and hailed to him and signalled to him to come.

The boy ran up the road gingerly, and received the letter, and both he and the Post Mistress laughed. Then he sped up the hill to his home.

The family huddled together to read the letter. The children, including Leroy, read with difficulty, because the words were long and they had not learnt them yet. But it was not long before the mother finished and she went back to the kitchen. Then she went back out to the children and she said, 'I don't think he said exactly when he'll come but it won't be long now. Let me see. . . .' She took the letter away and went into the kitchen. And she said to herself: 'Oh, is so? England nice. Trinidad too backward. He playing man already. Okay, let him stay there. We'll live without him.' And she called out, 'Leroy, go and give the goats water!'

The Stranger in the Village

❦❦❦

Today, when Eileen came in for the school mails, we chatted and laughed about the stranger in the village. In fact, ever since I left school and was shoved into this village Post Office, Eileen became my main fount of gossip, giving me tips of all that happened in the village. Not that very much happened in Tamana.

About the stranger, well he just appeared, as if from nowhere. I was one of the first to see him because he came here to ask for letters. He seemed a pleasant young man and really I do not know why Eileen found him so ridiculous. I thought he was all right, except that he never seemed to be concerned with one thing at one time. He would ask for letters but his eyes would be in the road outside, or looking about him, or looking at me, instead of at the letter cubicles. Today I said to Eileen, 'Perhaps he's some sweet-man'.

She laughed. She said, 'But nobody know where he come from. I hear some of my pupils say he must be from Sangre Grande, but I know Grandie and he ain't from there. And he's always dressed up, sporting about. Yesterday you remember when he come in asking for letters and he was talking about the heat? Now what so special about this heat!'

I nodded in agreement with Eileen although I'm not sure that I really agreed. If there's any place hotter than Tamana it must be the place next to hell. I don't know if I feel this way because I'm cooped up here, in this Post Office.

I said, 'This dry season doesn't make joke, girl.'

'I know, Post, but this feller only want to talk nonsense with you.'

'You think so?' My heart began to race. I couldn't wait for him to come here again to let me hear what nonsense he had to talk.

I finished stamping the letters and I placed them in their cubicles, setting aside those for Eileen's school. I turned round to her, a look of disgust on my face: 'You think he's a feller like that?'

'But you could see. One look and you could see he's a smart-man. Sometimes he does pass by the school and look in. Looking for what? I don't know. Post, I already suspect him.'

I held back Eileen's letters and went on talking to her. She was looking past me and at the letters as though she wanted to go, but I wanted to find out as much as I could.

I said, 'But this man is a mystery man. To think that nobody ain't know anything about him.'

'Not a single thing. Anyway, Post, girl, I think I have to run back.'

I handed her the mails reluctantly. I always liked talking to Eileen, but more so now. Eileen is an old school friend and we always gossiped. I always knew the boys who were chasing her – except when they were chasing me, too. She's still gossipy with me although she stayed on at school to be a teacher and I moved here from that world.

I said, 'Okay, then. See you. I have a hunch this feller is from somewhere in Port of Spain.'

'From Port of who? Who will leave Port of Spain to come here!'

'You don't know – perhaps it have a nice girl here.'

For a moment Eileen's pair of eyes and mine made four, framed against the door, against the houses outside, and against the redness of the immortelle hills. Then she burst out laughing and in a moment she was gone.

Whenever the man came in for letters these days he arrived either just before Eileen or just after her – so we were lucky to be able to talk quite freely about him. But one day he turned up quite unexpectedly while we were both talking . . . and we stiffened up and were silent, like two statues. Then Eileen took up her letters and skedaddled. The man said to me, 'Any letters?' He was looking straight at me instead of at the letter cubicles.

I said, 'No letters.' There were never any letters for him. I did not even look, because I knew.

'No letters, eh?' he said. But he did not seem to mind. Then he turned around looking out into the street. The sun was scorching down outside and it seemed as though he was now only taking refuge in the shade. I wondered why he was in so much of a hurry to go, these days.

Suddenly he turned back to the counter. He said, 'They call you "Post"?'

'Yes, but my name is Margaret.' My heart was thumping. He was looking at me but I did not want my eyes to meet his. I kept looking between him and the other half of the door, out into the road.

After a few moments he followed my gaze and turned his head again towards the road. 'This weather!' he said, 'This dry season, eh! The pitch like soft candle.'

Looking out at the pitch you could see the heat steaming up from it. You could see it in the way the air trembled over the surface. Every day around noontime it was like this. Blistering hot. Even from the Post Office you could see the pitch, soft from the sun and shining

128

as if it were a sheet of oil and not road at all. The cuteness of his remark made me smile.

He went on, 'This Tamana is a funny place.'

'Why?' This just slipped out of me. Right away I wanted to know why. Strangers were always finding places funny – except the places they came from.

He said, 'You can't see? Look out there. Nobody at all. Not a soul. Not even children. Or g. . . .' He stopped.

'Or what?'

'Not even children,' he said.

'But they at school.'

'I know – but still – you know.' Then he said, apologetically, 'To be honest, Tamana is nice.' I liked the way he said that. Just as I was going to add to his words he said, 'See you,' and slipped out.

The man continued coming to the Post Office and I must confess I always looked forward to seeing him. Still I did not know what he was or what brought him here and he was not quick to talk about that. Once, to Eileen, I faked a slip of the tongue and instead of calling him 'the stranger in the village,' I called him 'the danger in the village.' Eileen had a field day. She opened her eyes wide, and she put her hands to her mouth, and we had a good laugh.

Eileen herself had changed a great deal. She did not make conversation about the man now and in some ways it was as though she had had enough of the subject. These days she came to the Post Office only occasionally, and when she did not come one of her pupils came to collect the letters.

And just when I began to think about the stranger more and more, he, too, stopped coming. He disappeared from my routine just as suddenly as he had entered it, and I soon began to forget about him.

It must have been months afterwards, when, leaning against the counter and hoping someone would call for letters and ease the boredom, my thoughts suddenly fell on the stranger. The rainy season had already set in, but this day was hot and bright, and perhaps it was the new strangeness of this that brought the memory of the man back to me.

I remained some time with my heart, dreaming, feeling a little pain. Then the girl who called these days for the letters, appeared and I light-heartedly looked forward to a little conversation to change my train of thought.

'Hm! Thank goodness no rain today,' I said.

'No,' she said. She was very young and she looked shy and this gave me more confidence to speak with her.

I said, 'Wish I was still going to school, and free. It's like a prison behind this old counter.'

'Still, it cool here,' she said.

'You mean *cooler*. It hot outside?'

'If!'

The way she said this made me laugh and she chuckled, too. I said: 'Thought you was shy.'

She laughed.

'Tell your teacher she should at least come now and then. That's my pal, you know – old Eileen. What about her these days?'

The girl hesitated a little and then she said, 'Don't know.'

'Thought you was taking the letters for her. She doesn't teach your class still?'

The girl looked at me in a puzzled way and then she said, 'Teacher Eileen doesn't teach now. At least not here.'

'Doesn't teach? *Eileen?*' I half believed she did not know who I was talking about.

The girl looked at me and then she looked to see if

anybody was coming into the Post Office. Then she whispered, 'You don't know about it, Post? Really?'

'About what?' It was my turn to look puzzled.

The girl looked embarrassed and smiled. She was more confused and shy than ever. 'Oh, well, you see,' she said, 'It's a few weeks now, you know. I mean, the feller who was here. The feller we used to call "the stranger". Well, he and Eileen went away together. You know.'

With her letters in hand she moved uneasily towards the door, then down the steps and then she was out in the road.

It was very hot. Blistering hot. The heat seemed to be choking me at this moment. Turning away, I unhung the calendar from the wall and began fanning. I let out a big 'Whew!' for the heat. And with that 'Whew!' all the shock of my bewilderment and disappointment was let loose. At that moment I felt calm inside and I was thankful for many things. For one thing, I was thankful for my quiet life here, dull, cooped up, but safe. I shook my head. I really liked this stool, from which I could watch the weather changing, and the people changing even faster than the weather. And I was thankful, too, for being made to realize that Tamana was not such a dull place after all.

The Sword of the Trespasser

❖❖❖

The great Cacique was troubled. There was unrest among the tribe. He did not know how long he could hold them back – how long he could keep them peaceful. For they were the Achtura – the fire-blooded Caribs. They had almost wiped out the Arawaks completely and now there were very few more for them to turn on. But with the rising of the moon the war-cries would rend the air again.

The great Chief had counselled with the tribe for a long time and they had listened silently, for they respected – almost feared – this wise one. For through many moons, moons long spent, he had been Dreamer and Leader of the tribe. And he had guided them well and had explained many things. He had even explained about the great fire that travelled right across the skies and burned on the sea at evenings. So there was nothing he did not understand. Nothing.

But his pleadings for peacefulness had brought dismay upon the tribe. Warring had been in their bodies, in their very blood. They felt they could not give it up. Having devoured the defenceless Arawaks they were now planning to cross the Iëre seas. There was a mainland where the ill-fated Arawaks had sailed from. One of the victims had given all the details of that place. For a while they had spared his life because he would be a good guide,

132

but soon afterwards they devoured him, too. Now they wanted to build canoes to cross the Iëre seas.

These things greatly distressed the Cacique, and especially so as he had had a strange dream. For he had dreamt of ducks. A swarm of red-billed sea-ducks that came from the sunrise ocean. His drums had called the chieftains from every corner of the coast, but when they heard the news they were overjoyed.

Strangers coming here from the ocean! they thought. For they, too, knew the meaning of this dream.

The Cacique had not mentioned anything of the red bills. In his dream the red had been brighter than war-paint. He knew what the red meant. The last time he had dreamt of red-billed sea-ducks he had seen what had befallen the mainland strangers. He did not want to see any more blood and he had grown sick of the flesh-feasts. But the chieftains had listened with hungering lips and with their fingers trembling on their bows.

'No more fighting!' the old man had said, in the coarse, guttural language of the tribe. 'No more killing!'

It was his usual talk. The chieftains could not tell what was wrong with him. They had called him 'The Strange One'. He was indeed a strange one, with strange thoughts, and with silver hairs falling onto his shoulders. Of the tribe, he was the only one with silver hair, for he had been among them for many moons. The long, jet-black hair of the rest never had time to silver – for they were the Achtura, the death-dealing ones.

The old Cacique, with his skin flabby and wrinkled now, but with eyes still like a hawk's, came to the beach often to look out on the sea. He knew that he was the strange and weird-looking one but he wanted to be good to his tribe and at the same time to protect the sea-people. For they would come, and from the sunrise.

He spoke again to his chieftains – many times – and

they had watched him and wondered about him. Deep down they knew he was right. They knew of his guidance and his great protection. Sometimes they had held him to be half Cacique, half God. And at other times, unsettled by silver hairs and dark brown shoulders they had known him to be all God and were in awe of him. This was mainly why he had managed to hold the tribe together for so long. Not that he could control their war-passion. But now he could stand no more blood.

'No fighting,' he had said in the harshness of his Carib tongue, 'When the sea-people come, no more killing here. Plenty other food. Plenty lappa, plenty tamayoc. No more blood!' He had fixed them with his gaze but even so he could see the restless, twitching fingers, the head-veins swollen as though they would burst.

Once he shouted, enraged, 'No more!' For he could see what thoughts possessed them. And then he had made the threat. He had threatened to take his own life if they feasted on the sea-people. They had shrunk back. If he did that, the terrible curse would be upon them. The Cacique had walked off then, much shaken.

And sure enough one morning the sea-ducks arrived. The canoes from the sunrise were riding just off the coast. Christoforo Colombo with his ships had cast anchor.

Christoforo standing on deck with spying-glass, scanned the coast before him. It looked as peaceful as it was beautiful and green. Yet who was he to trust! Who was he to forget the warlike Caribs that had attacked from Guanahani to Xamaica, on both of the other voyages! He looked long at the wide freshwater stream and once more he was tempted to send a boat ashore. He strained his eyes at the coast. The forests were thick, but where he could see between the leaves he could see nothing. He lifted his eyes to the mountain peaks and he repeated, 'La Trinidad'. Then he lifted his eyes to heaven and his heart became full.

Only yester-evening, as the sun set, he had dedicated this land to the Trinity. He had sighted the three peaks even from the ocean and falling on his knees he had claimed this land for God and for Spain. For he knew that he had travelled so far only because God had been with him.

And yet he would not land, because he was not trusting. He peered long through his spying-glass but there was no sign of life on the green coast. His men were impatient. They were thirsting to death and there was a river before them but he would not give them permission to approach the shore. Not yet. He held his face in his hands and murmured a prayer. Then he lifted his spying-glass again.

And seeing the clear, wide river he felt as if a shaft of light burst through his mind. It was a miracle that brought them here. It was a miracle that led them across the seas to this strange land. His men were thirsting to death and it was a miracle that brought them to this stream. Then would the miracle let them perish? Christoforo Colombo laughed at himself. Then he turned round to his men and cried, 'The boats! Lower the boats!'

Wild, delirious voices echoed, 'Lower the boats. . . . The boats. . . .'

Then the admiral went to his log to enter the command. Above the page his trembling fingers scrawled '31st July, 1498'.

The thirsting, parched-tongued Spaniards were wild with the joy of fresh water. They leaned over in the little boats and put their mouths to the river and drank, and then they laughed aloud with the free, vulgar laugh of

135

adventurers. They sank their kegs below the river's surface then brought them up again, full, and dripping. After they had filled every one, they lay back in the boats and looked at the sun, and then they wanted to go and lie down on the beach and sleep.

But then they remembered the Captain's spying-glass and they did not want to seem careless. But they were as happy as children. They sailed just a little way up the river – for the river could not be very deep – and running the boat against the sand they came out and lazed near the river's edge in the sun.

This went on for some time and fits of hot and cold swept over the watching Caribs. But not a leaf stirred in the trees. With hungry eyes and half-crazed minds they glared at the sea-people and their bellies tumbled inside them and their hands shook as with the ague.

But the threat of the great Cacique was like iron fingers tearing them away. They looked at the red cheeks and the fleshy legs stretched out in the sun and they licked their lips and sweated. But the Cacique could not be defied. If he took his own life the Spirits would haunt the tribe for a thousand years.

They groaned aloud as the Spaniards rowed back to sea.

The great Cacique walked down to the river himself because it had been reported that the sea-people had been there. The angry warriors had said that the sea-people had come to make war. They had said this because they wanted the Cacique to get angry, for the sea-people looked very good for eating. The last tribe from the sea had flesh that was stringy. These sea-people looked tender and very delicious. The big, strange canoes were still in the bay. The warriors were sure that the little canoes would leave the big canoes and come to the river again. They wanted the Wise One to get angry and call for war-paint.

But the Wise One was determined there should be no blood. Now in the evening sunlight he sat down by the river. He had already forbidden the place to his warriors. As he waited he thought of the dream.

His dreams never failed to work out. Did the sea-people really come to make war? The red bills of the ducks in his dream troubled him. He had dreamt the same thing just before the last, ill-fated strangers had come. But they had not come in war. It was his own tribe that had caused the massacre. Oh how they relished flesh like their own flesh! He had to hold them back now. He had to break them back and teach them.

He sat with the sun sinking and waited. Many-coloured hummingbirds buzzed about him. Beside him were strings of tamayoc, and ocras, and a long stem of the jointed grass. And he had brought maize, also. He looked down at the river and in the river he saw the reflection of himself with the full feathers of the Cacique of the tribe. If the sea-people came in war he would make peace offerings and they would go away.

Christoforo Colombo, on being told of the calmness of the isle, went ashore that evening. The admiral had a shock. First, on arriving on the beach, he and his men were startled to see a Carib by the river. He drew his sword and ran into the bushes after the Carib. He rushed back blowing and jumped into the boat, and they pushed off desperately from the river-bank. They rowed hard for the galleon in the bay.

And now the Captain dipped his sword in the sea-water. Blood, red and thick, oozed down from the hilt. The Captain's head reeled. Only this morning he had promised God. . . . He had promised – Remorse choked him. 'Holy Virgin!' he cried.

The Precious Corn

❀❀❀

The watchman was up early. He had hardly slept. All night he had listened to the wind raging. Now he hurried out to see what had happened to the corn.

And what had happened pained his heart. The wind had hit the entire east side of the field. It didn't uproot the trees but it had ravaged them. The watchman felt agony in him and fought to steady himself.

The damage was wide. There was a full day's work in it. It was better to set about it right away. Bending down he straightened one of the trees gently and scraped the rich, black soil around the roots. Then he rammed the soil firmly in with a piece of stick. He watched the long, green blades and the bright tassle and he stood up and felt to see the place where the cob was forming. It was pitiful. These were the young trees that hadn't produced yet. The wind had left the others and hit the young trees.

Yet this was just coincidence. On the whole the wind was no enemy. It had very seldom struck. He couldn't even recall the last time it had damaged his corn. He had never feared the wind.

It was the corn thieves he feared. Or, the corn thief, rather. He didn't know if there were others but he was sure of this one. The man who lived at the far end of the cornfield was the real dagger in his side. The trees near the house were always stripped of corn. Whenever he passed nearby there was always the smell of roasting

corn in the air. But this man had never put a grain in
the soil. This was the real enemy he had to contend with.
Day and night he had planned to catch the man. But not
one of his traps worked. So he consoled himself by walking with the little stick. The little stick had a big knot
at one end. That was the only trap he had left. If he
caught the man red-handed he wouldn't lose his corn
any more.

He was scraping earth now around another tree. About
half a dozen trees were already put erect. There was a
long line of blown down ones stretching to the distance.
The watchman stood up again and surveyed the task.
It was a tremendous one and not one to brood over.
He pulled a deep breath in and clenched his teeth.

It was true that the back of the man's house opened
on the cornfield. Or, as the man regarded it, the cornfield
stretched up to his house. By nature he was far from
being a thief, but the hard times and the asthma, and
the plenty that flourished beside him, would have tested
even stronger men.

Especially if they liked corn as he did. Often, breathing
heavily with the sickness which kept him from work, he
crept out among those trees, hastily breaking the ears of
corn and dropping them into the little bag. And he crept
back into his house again on hands and knees, looking
uneasily about him and thanking heaven he wasn't seen.
For he was jealous of his good name and even as he lit
the coal fire his conscience would trouble him a little.
But the vastness of the plantation reassured him. A few
ears of corn would make not the slightest difference to
that abundant harvest.

He, too, had heard the storm during the night. With
the first light he had looked out of the window. He had
seen the big dent in the far side of the field, so he knew

that for many days it would be safe at his end. He was sorry in a way for the watchman. For much of the corn would be lost. But even so it was not the watchman's corn. That was why when he took the corn he did not feel too badly. The corn belonged to Sanderson, and Sanderson was so wealthy that his wealth corrupted him. He was the vilest man alive. News had gone around that when the watchman complained about the corn being stolen, Sanderson threatened to sack him, saying he employed him to protect the corn. This was wicked, but in a way it was good. It was good because the watchman wouldn't complain to Sanderson any more. Still he didn't trust the watchman. He seemed the sort that would do anything.

The man had watched the crippled trees again and it had come to his embittered mind that the destruction wasn't wide enough. For Sanderson was corrupt and his watchman was stupid.

It seemed strange, then, that the corn should prosper. But prosper it did. The man smiled whimsically. Life was really a puzzle. No corn was bigger or sweeter than Sanderson's corn. And as he thought of this he was more conscious of the emptiness in his stomach. And he looked at the field just outside and could hardly wait for night to fall.

All day the watchman laboured. He straightened and moulded the trees that could be straightened and moulded and he chopped away those broken by the wind. The heaps of chopped-away trees were bright with tassle and with the hair of young corn. The watchman worked on, fighting his agony.

He worked till the darkness came down. Then it wasn't safe to be using a cutlass. The trouble was enough as it was. He stood up and his eyes took in the whole field. There was no other corn plantation he knew of that was so vast. In the distance the long blades curved high and bushily and the brownness of the mature cobs could be seen in the little spaces. He wondered what it was in his hands that the corn should flourish so. He wondered if it was just experience. In this line experience was a key thing. You had to have experience and you had to love working with corn. After every crop he manured and forked up every inch of this field. Then he let the soil rest a little. And when he knew the soil was ready he put the very best seeds in. Then, with a little rain and a little care the shoots sprouted to his hands and grew up like his own children.

He could not have loved his own children as he loved this corn. He put the cutlass in the tool shed and taking the stick, more by habit, he walked a little in the gloom.

As he walked along the side of the field he looked fondly at the trees that had withstood the wind. Some leaned only the slightest bit and they were all right. And as he approached the far side the trees were not touched at all. He prodded some of them with his stick although he knew they were not touched, and at times he used the big knot of the stick and tested them.

And he thought of how the wind had worried him through the night. The damage had not been beyond him. He had almost finished putting things right. He still had energy to work all day and undo what the great wind had done. He was a little pleased with himself.

He was on the point of turning back when a shuffle in the corn startled him. There was the small movement of a shadow. Then everything was still. It took only those movements to transform him. The blood rushed to his head. Corn thief! he thought. Corn thief! And he felt his brain pounding against his head. The shadow was still, thinking itself unlocated. But the watchman moved cruelly into the corn. He was strong even without

141

anger, and the big knot of his stick blistered cornleaf and struck heavily where the shadow had stirred.

'O, God!'

The cry was sharp and low and mixed with heavy breathing. The blows fell madly. The watchman's hands were like a windmill in their rage. He struck out in the darkness and, unappeased, he hit with everything he had in him. And at last his own breath came heavily. But the cries and the heavier breathing were already silenced. Panting, he looked at the stick. The big knot had broken off and there was a shiny substance where the knot had been. The watchman put his finger on it and the substance felt warm and wet. Looking at his fingers he saw the blood trickling across them.

He looked about him and then he walked away quickly. He flung the stick away. A new thought came into his mind now. He walked out not knowing exactly what he was going to do. His heart was thumping. He wondered if the man could crawl out and go. He did not want to think what kept coming into his head. He staggered hastily out of the corn.

There was no storm that night but the watchman could not sleep. Ghastly feelings wrestled with him and he tossed and turned and then he got up and dressed and went to the Police Station. There were no corn thoughts in his mind now. First there was wildness and now fear had set in. Nothing like this had ever happened in his life before. He went as a weak man to the police.

They came back with him, four of them. They did not take care to walk around the field for corn was not precious to them. They were needled because of the hour of the night and because of what this man had done. Nobody would come to the police station if they had just hit a corn thief a few light blows with a stick. They walked through the corn making a big, clear track before them, pushing the trees aside, trampling them. The lumps under their boots were the ears of corn and the ears of corn stuck in the mud. They spoke hostilely to the watchman asking him where the spot was exactly. There was feverishness in the watchman's eyes. When they came to the spot they flashed their torches on the man on the ground. Then something clinked in the dark as they slipped it onto the watchman's hand. Then three of them walked away with him while one remained to watch the corpse.